Pete

Enjoy the book
Mate

all the best

STEEL CITY PRESS

This first edition published in 2021 by Steel City Press,
9 Ravenscroft Close, Sheffield, S13 8PN.

The Non-Essential Worker
ISBN 978-1-913047-20-7

Copyright © 2021 Danny Posthill

Printed by TJ Books Limited

CONTENTS

CREDITS

John Tennant: Thank you for giving me the inspiration for writing this book. It just goes to show that a Zoom piss-up can bring out the best in people.

Dave Taylor: You have helped me along the way in this pandemic. Thank you for your regular support and advice when it comes to getting ideas together for sketches and various other projects, and thank you for giving me great honest feedback during the edit of this book before it went to print.

Aimee: You have stuck by me throughout lockdown. You have been my absolute rock. Even though we have had our disagreements during lockdown, as couples do, I couldn't have done this book or lockdown without you. You have spent endless hours massively helping with the editing of the book, and support me through everything I ever do in work and life. I am so thankful to have you by my side.

Everyone who has bought this book: It means so much to me, thank you all. I only decided to do this as a last-minute thing over a few drinks on a whim, as I do, and I am so glad that I did take this opportunity to pass on my story to you all. I hope you found some amusement amongst all the madness!

Paul Eastwood, Matt Bragg, Alan Francis, Joe Allon, Bobby Davro, Geoff Whiting, Jack Gleadow, Dave Watkin, Mike Swan, Rudi West, Kim and Anth Pugh, Andy and Laurie Smallwood, Simon and Rachel Hanlon, Mike Cox and Katie Bloor, Jamie Wetherill, Robbie Brown, Russ Kane, John Altman, Pam and Steve Gooderham, and to all my family that have been at the other end of the phone when I needed them...my mam Tracy Payne, Stepdad John Payne, Brother Tom Payne, Uncle Ian Payne, Alison, Mark, Matthew and Daniel, Auntie Linda Hamilton, cousins Ben and Tony Hamilton, Uncle and Auntie Paul and Angela Posthill, my Nana Pauline Posthill, cousins Joe and Amy Posthill, and my Auntie Sylvie: Thank you all for being there for me during the lockdowns, and for keeping me sane.

TESTIMONIAL

By Bobby Davro

I first saw Danny on Britain's Got Talent in 2015. I was so impressed by his talent for mimicry and impressions that I felt that I had to contact him via social media to tell him just how good I thought he was.

He was so original and contemporary with his voices and material, and to me it was a revelation. Since then we have become close friends and his dedication along with his enthusiasm for his craft has never diminished. I believe given the right opportunities he could become one of the finest comedy talents of our generation.

Enjoy this book as it represents everything comedians and entertainers have had to embrace and contend with throughout the Covid pandemic. I wish him well and every success. I always will remain his friend and supporter.

Foreword -
Why write a book?

"Why don't you write a book, Dan?"

I'm on a Zoom call to a friend of mine having a catch up and a drink – we've had plenty of them over lockdown let me tell you, especially the most recent one. Lockdown and Christmas are bad enough for your health separately, never mind putting them together.

Christmas is the worst for me when it comes to overindulging. Every New Year's Day I have to tell myself to stop living like an alcoholic and an obese person, otherwise I'll end up on a Channel 5 documentary. I'm on a detox now so all is good.

I responded to John "Everyone's writing books in lockdown". I say everyone, but I mean celebrities (yeah, I've done a tiny bit of TV but I wouldn't call myself a celebrity).

On second thoughts I didn't think writing a book was actually such a bad idea. I've been a full-time comedian since 2013 and I was earning a decent living – but then the pandemic hit. It's been a rollercoaster ride on many different levels and has been financially and mentally straining.

My mate John had a point. People are so nosey, they're gonna want to know more. I keep getting stopped by people who don't know me personally but like to ask me how I'm coping. They're talking like I just lost a relative or a friend and in a way I suppose I have. I'm mourning my loss of comedy. No, not comedy. Stand-up. You can't work the audience if there's no audience. There's nothing like the feeling of working live, so in a way people must have an inkling that it must be pretty tough for an entertainer who's not allowed to entertain. Why not write a book to dish the dirt?

I met John a few years back in a pub next door to the Borough Hall in Hartlepool, I sat and chatted with him for a bit and soon the conversation flowed quicker than the beers. I subtly crow-barred some new material in that I was going to do that night and he laughed. Us entertainers are needy people. We thrive off a bit of applause, so to be fair I'm always going to take a liking to anyone who laughs at my material. This gig was a corporate one for the Council, so the stuff I tried out on him was very bespoke. Basically, if you didn't live in Hartlepool you wouldn't have a clue what I was on about. We've become friends ever since.

So, me and John are having this Zoom chat during the third-and-hopefully-final lockdown. The booze is flowing so the conversation repeats itself and we start talking again about me writing a book. That's when I thought to myself, I've got nothing to lose so why not?

Plus, when I say I am going to do something I have to do it. I like to think that I am a man of my word. It's something I've always made a point of.

After one gig a lady told me about a charity she was involved in, so I told her I'd run a half-marathon to raise money. It seemed like a good idea after 6 pints of Thatcher's cider (Thatcher's cider is pretty much the only time you can use the word 'Thatcher' in Hartlepool and get away with it). When I woke up the next day with a hangover, I thought to myself "Why did I say I would do a half-marathon?". Anyway to cut a long story short, I'm a man of my word so I did the half-marathon.

I'm keeping my drunken promise to write a book too. It's 1:30 in the afternoon, January 2nd 2021. I was planning to start writing on January 1st, but like many of us I was just too hungover so I ate unhealthy food and watched Netflix instead. Last year was tough, not just for me but for the whole of the entertainment industry. I feel like we've been neglected and forgotten about, left to struggle through alone.

I'm going to take you on a journey through my life in comedy and a year of battling through lockdowns, being deprived of doing a job I love. Since Covid became the newest and pretty much most-used word in the dictionary, people have been offering me helpful advice like "why don't you get a normal job then?", or "Retrain as something else, entertainment isn't going to come back for ages". The one I think I heard the most was "Well Dan if you got a trade you would have been safe and you would have been an essential worker". Yeah, thanks for that.

For myself and everyone else in the entertainment industry we always knew our careers wouldn't always be stable but we wanted to follow our passion. Our work being completely taken away by a global pandemic was something that none of us could have predicted.

As far as I am concerned, I have got a trade, which is the refined art of making people laugh. That also requires failing a number of times before you can succeed. When you fail in comedy it hurts ten times more than if you fail in most other jobs, because you make yourself look like a right dick. It's then up to you to go back to the drawing board to put it right.

Then when you do nail it, you eventually have material that flows. The buzz you get from it is just unexplainable, the best feeling ever! I can't say it's better than sex, because my other half Aimee is probably going to read this and she'd get a bit annoyed at that analogy. I can just hear her now, telling me that if comedy's better than sex, why don't I go and find an audience then? I'd be pretty screwed, if you'll excuse the pun. Oh, and my in-laws will see this bit too...sorry Mark and Alison. Me and Aimee have been together for 8 years and we are still going strong.

The girl who stands by me throughout

So yes, I've had a few 'normal jobs' before taking on comedy full-time. For now, as you can see I am currently retraining as an author even though I only got a 'C' in GCSE English.

I would like to thank my good mate Dave Taylor for proofreading this. I remember calling him up and telling him about my idea of writing a book, what I should call it, and to ask him if he would proofread it for me. His response was, "I think it's a great idea…asking someone who is more intelligent than you to proofread the book." Cheeky bastard. He's also a good friend and I run a lot of ideas past him because he's honest; a true mate never lies to you. I met Dave when he auditioned me for a season on a cruise ship and we've been mates ever since.

Anyway, enjoy the book and I hope you all like it.

Episode 1 - The News

I honestly didn't think COVID-19 would be that bad. It was happening in China on the news, but I never thought it would get this far. I was sitting around doing nothing and scrolling on my Instagram news feed, when I saw a friend's video in what would normally be a busy area of China. It looked like a ghost town. I couldn't believe what I was seeing. Being an optimistic person by nature, I thought to myself, "well if China is in a lockdown and they're dealing with this virus, surely it won't spread any further".

A few weeks went by and then it started spreading to other countries. Now I started to worry. There were so many questions going through my head. How bad is this virus? Will it wipe the world out? But the biggest one which sticks with us all today: how did it start? There was talk at first that it came from a bat. That one had to be total bollox because I saw a Facebook meme with a picture of Ozzy Osbourne saying "If this disease came from bats then how come I haven't got COVID-19? I bit a bat's head off in 1982!"

Can't argue with Facebook logic. Sorry, I can't put an emoji at the end of that sentence to explain I'm taking the piss. I must write this book the posh way and show no emotion when I am writing a sentence. This is like a *Proper Book*, and I have to act like an author now. I'm not just some comedian on Facebook with shit grammar and emojis at the end of his sentences just to soften the blow for the easily offended. It's a puzzle. You've got to figure out the emojis for yourself.

Speaking of grammar, I once had a Twitter stalker who was constantly messaging me. That is pretty flattering and a great ego boost, but there are limits. This was pretty much ten times a day. I messaged back and said "Hi this is Danny's partner, I look after his twitter account, so sorry we haven't responded as we have been really busy on other projects".

I thought that should give her the hint and soften the blow a little bit. Her response was "Ah, so you're the one with the shit grammar!" - and of course Aimee was really offended because she is the one who corrects my grammar, and has spent endless hours doing just that on this book.

According to the news Covid-19 was spreading like wildfire. There were loads of people dying, hospitals were full and then boom! Before we knew it Boris was on the news, making live announcements and telling us all that cases have been discovered in the UK. This is where shit got serious for me, what will happen now? I had a diary full of gigs and I thought if this all kicks off, I'm going to be left with no work, I've still got a mortgage, bills and overheads to pay.

I know what you're thinking after reading that sentence. "People have lost their lives and all you can think about is not being on stage for a while…you selfish bastard!" That's the thing about this virus though. It affects people in different ways. Some people will obviously suffer physically, but others will struggle with their mental health during lockdown too. People will lose money and their livelihoods, sending them into a downward spiral which can be pretty depressing. Being skint is awful at the best of times.

The worst financial situation I have been in was when I was 19. I headed out to Majorca on a whim (not a drunken bet for once) to try and be a professional comic. A Spanish agent saw me in a working men's club in Nottingham and decided to book me to go and live out there for a few months. I'd been performing in a few clubs, singing a few songs and doing a bit of comedy. I was doing more vocal impressions then, of people like Ronan Keating, Neil Diamond, and Tony Christie.

This Spanish agent couldn't speak a word of English. He decided that the audience liked me, so he gave me a 6-month contract to go out and do the hotels in Majorca. I felt like a total legend, and couldn't wait to tell all my mates. About two months later when I got out there, I was picked up at the airport by an Elvis Presley tribute, who could speak Spanish and was also at the original gig at the club in Nottingham. He had reassured the agent at the time that I was a good act.

Unfortunately the agent was sending me to gigs that were unplayable. Even with the experience that I have now, I would still struggle. He sent me to one gig where I was doing my act, and got nothing back, 'dying on my arse' as they call it in the showbiz world. I said to the audience "This is clearly not working and I'm clearly not for you, so I think it's best I don't disturb your evening any longer."

However, there was a call from the back of the room from a guy who said, "Keep going mate, me and the missus are loving it. They don't know what you're talking about, they're all German and Swedish." Most Swedish and German people speak very good English, and to be fair I tend to think that us English can be ignorant in the sense that many of us never bother to learn another language.

By chance, in this case the audience didn't speak a word of English. Yes, the agent had got me a gig at a hotel that didn't cater for English tourists and thought it was a good idea to put on an English comedian. I was fighting a losing battle.

This happened a few times. Within weeks I'd lost so many gigs that I couldn't afford to pay my rent, so I got kicked out of my apartment. Looking back, I wasn't that experienced. If I could see my act again today, even I'd probably say it was shit. Fortunately, a few weeks previously I had already taken a day job at a hotel as an entertainer, keeping the guests entertained between 10am and 5pm. I had breaks of course, doing activities such as carpet bowls, killer darts and so on.

That job was a blessing really because when I got kicked out of my apartment, I had a key for the activities room. It had a shower, a few pieces of gym equipment, and a sauna. That was the closest thing I had to a plan: I'd keep my case and belongings in the van I was hiring, and have a shower and get ready in the games room at my day job. I would have to make sure to lock the door behind me, and leave the key in the lock, so that I could have a bit of privacy and no one would walk in and catch me showering at work.

That was Day 1 of survival. 'Danny Bear Grylls Posthill' goes off into the big wide world, slumming it, with very little money, and doesn't tell his mam because she'd be worried sick. To be fair, I've always liked a challenge. Before this I'd been living at home with my parents, with a meal on the table every night, a roof over my head, and paying my mam about 20 quid a week. Bargain.

This new way of life was on a whole other level. I planned to switch between the van and the hotel for another two months, all whilst trying to not get caught by the manager Helen, who I happened to get on really well with. My plan of action was working well enough. I had my shower, got changed, did my shift, finished my shift, then ended up having a drink at the bar with these Italian guys who were guests at the hotel. They kept pumping me full of booze, and they also couldn't speak much English, but we seemed to get on really well.

At this moment I could have been down and depressed at the events that had unfolded over the past week, but there's something about being 19, in sun-drenched Majorca, and completely pissed with two strangers. I thought to myself that I should be able to survive this for 2 months, no problem.

At 1am I decided that it was bedtime. I headed to the games room, which was no larger than a standard living room. It was all dark and dingy, with the only windows being the Mediterranean-style ones on the top of the wall just below the ceiling. At the back of the room there was a wooden door which led to a sauna and shower, which was always kept immaculately clean. I locked the main door behind me, and thought where can I sleep? The floor was tiled, just like in every other Spanish building, it didn't look very welcoming to rest my head on. It was either that or sleep in my van, and that seemed too dangerous.

Someone once told me that if you sleep on a wooden flat surface it's good for your back. I'll believe any old shit people tell me, so I took sleeping in the sauna as a positive (it wasn't on obviously). I lay down to try to get some sleep. No chance. No pillow. The closest thing I could find was a costume of the hotel's mascot, which just happened to be an elephant.

I strip down to my pants, put the elephant's head on and go to sleep in my new rent-free apartment.

The elephant's actually pretty comfortable, with a big mouth (appropriate, I thought) so I can breathe. After a few drinks at night I'm out like a light…

No alarm clock needed. I'm woken up by a massive scream. It's the cleaner, who's clearly traumatised by the experience. I can't say I'm surprised. She must have thought I was dead. If I was dead, why would I die with an elephant's head on? Some kind of kinky sex game gone wrong? There must have been so many questions going through that poor woman's head. I tried to calm her down, but the language barrier didn't help. How could I explain why a half-naked man was wearing an elephant's head and sleeping in a sauna?

Helen, the hotel manager, was a very strong and proud woman who ran a really tight ship. She called me into her office. "Danny", she asked, "why did you sleep in the sauna?" Thankfully, she didn't add the elephant bit or the half-naked bit. It was embarrassing enough as it was. I explained that it was either sleeping in the sauna or the van, and she took pity on me because it was so obvious that I was really struggling. She liked me, and the scores were up for entertainment in the hotel, so she decided to give me a room for free for the rest of the season. I couldn't have thanked her enough, I was and still am so grateful.

The hotel was in a tranquil area of Alcudia, and the rooms in the hotel were really nice. I even managed to blag myself free meals every day from the restaurant that was attached to the hotel. I was encouraging all the guests to eat there, so I was drumming up extra business for them. It was all good, plus I still had a couple of gigs booked in that were for the English-speaking hotels. I wasn't in a bad position in the end. The moral of the story is, when you're at an all-time low, find a solution, and think positively. No matter how bad it is, eventually something good will happen.

Also, this is me learning my trade. If anyone thinks that doing stand-up comedy or being an entertainer is not a trade, you can fuck right off. (Sorry Nana, I did warn you there's a little bit of swearing in this!) The funny thing is my mates were at home doing their day jobs which brought them more security. They were moaning about doing a 12-hour shift whilst they thought I was in the sun drinking cocktails living the life of Riley. They had no idea.

It seems to be one thing after another with me. I get myself into situations such as the sauna fiasco, but always find my way out.Fortunately I did sleep in the sauna. If I'd slept in my van, I could imagine knowing my luck that the Spanish police would have ended up getting involved. That wouldn't have been my first run-in with the Guardia Civil.

I'd already got pulled over by them for drink-driving. It was pretty stupid, and I'm not exactly proud of it, but I know you're all nosey bastards who want to know things like this.

My agent bought me drink after drink one night, and I said "I'm off to get a taxi". I'd had quite enough: if drinking alcohol was a sport, I was the local village player training with a world champion. I couldn't keep up. He told me, in his broken and now slightly-slurred English, "Is ok Danny, in Majorca we all drink drive". Toni was a nice guy and he did look after me, but that was the shittest advice in the history of advice.

Believing his charm, I stupidly jumped into my van and started driving it back. I was barely a mile down the road when I saw the Guardia Civil randomly pulling people over and breathalysing them. I'm not sure what it was about driving a banged-up old rental van that made them stop me, but of course I was pulled over. You never get away with things in those situations.

Of course I was well over the limit and the policeman asked me how much I had to drink. I was so petrified to the point where if I shat myself there and then I wouldn't have been surprised, but I tried to make it look like I was confident. I replied to his question, "10 vodka cola light". You what? He looked pretty shocked and asked me to repeat it. "10 vodka cola light", I said again.

"How is it possible to have that much to drink, and then drive?", he asked. Thinking back now, I'm sure he probably didn't intend it as a compliment, but after ten vodkas I took it that way. At least I was good at something. I'm not particularly proud of my reply, but at least it was funny. "I managed to drive and have 10 vodkas and cola light because I had a line of cocaine to wake me up"

The policeman laughed his head off. It was a joke of course! At the time I saw myself as a rebel, because I particularly admire rebellious comedians. I admired George Carlin and Billy Connolly so much, because they didn't care who they upset. But then again, they were in a good enough financial position to do so.

Not only did the policeman laugh, he turned round to his three other colleagues and translated it to them in Spanish. They all laughed their heads off too. I always push my luck and use humour to get myself out of the shit, and I thought great stuff Dan you've gotten away with this. That was right up to the point where the officer turned to me and said "Okay, 420 euros and you can go"

"What?"

"You give me 420 euros and you can go"

"I have no money, no dinero"

Okay", he replied.

Was I going to get away with this scot-free? No. He jumped in the passenger seat and said the words that I will never forget:

"Drive me to the cash machine".

I mean, what the fuck? This joker pulls me over for drink-driving and then tells me to drive him to a cash machine? I'm supposed to be under the influence and a danger to myself and others, but he didn't mind jumping in a car with me so that he could take a back-hander. I mean, wow. That really takes some getting your head around.

We got to the cash machine, and I didn't have 420 euros in my account, so he took my van off me. I could have the van back when I paid him the 420 euros. Great. Toni paid the fine the next day, then deducted it from the few gigs I had left for him.

Being a comedian can be a huge strain financially, especially when you are starting out. That's why I had to tell you these stories, to help give you a deeper understanding of my struggles, as entertaining as they might be. When Covid-19 came along, I didn't want to get myself into financial difficulty again. I've worked hard and taken a lot of shit over the years to get to where I am now. It would be a damn shame to be back at square one from something that is no fault of my own. But positivity is a huge factor, and it has got me through many things.

Aimee, my wife, says that I can sometimes be too optimistic. That means I can be a bit of a nutter and do some crazily stupid things, like the time I decided to jump off the Strat (a hotel, casino and sky pod which has the tallest free-standing observation tower in the USA) in Las Vegas in order to overcome my fear of heights. At the top of the tower there is a tourist attraction 'sky jump', and it's a 253-metre drop. I was strapped to a bungee, obviously, otherwise I wouldn't be here, but Aimee worried that the bungee would snap. I didn't stop bragging about it. The next day me and Aimee were going to the same building for dinner, at the 'Top of the World' restaurant, and there I was in the lift full of people telling them all that I jumped off the Strat.

Still can't believe
I jumped

As I was telling the whole lift they seemed quite impressed, until the elevator operator (or lift person, in English), decided to let me know that he jumped off the Strat 7 times. He had also done 8 sky dives. He didn't stop there, listing all these wild things he had done, half of which we had never heard of, so I interrupted him - and simply said in my Hartlepool way, "Alright mate you win!" Everyone in the lift laughed. I learned a very valuable lesson that day: no one likes a bragger.

A friend of mine, who was dating Aimee's best friend, set me up on a date with Aimee. That sounds like the plot of pretty much every romantic sitcom ever, but it worked for us. "I think you would really like him", Aimee's friend told her, "he's lovely". If I'm honest I value her opinion highly. Well who doesn't value the opinion of someone who says nice things about them?

Aimee added me on Facebook, we got talking, exchanged numbers and started to speak over the phone. We would be on the phone for hours and it never seemed to get dull. There were no awkward pauses and the conversation just flowed. After a few weeks we decided to meet up as I was flying back into Gatwick after doing a gig in Majorca. She was living down South at the time, studying at vocational college training as a dancer, so it was a great opportunity to meet up.

We'd never met before, so I couldn't exactly demand to stay at her place. That would be creepy. I was going to book a hotel, but she surprised me by inviting me to stay overnight. Wow, bloody hell she's keen, I thought. But then she also said "yeah, you can stay in the spare room", which made me realise that I was jumping to conclusions. She asked "What do you want to do then, shall we go out for a meal or shall I just cook for us?"

Tough decision. I mean, she was already letting me stay at her flat so I was saving money on a hotel. I could be all classy and take her out to wine and dine her. But instead I said "Why don't I bring a cheap bottle of vodka back from duty free at the airport and you cook for us?"

She laughed at first, thinking I was joking, but then to my surprise said "yeah, alright". You know how people say they have this earth-shattering moment when they know they've met the person they're meant to spend the rest of their lives with? My first thought was "she's a keeper". I mean what a date! A night away from home, a full meal and a night of drinks for two – and all it cost me was 14 euros from the airport duty free.

The date was a success and let's just say that I didn't sleep in the spare room that night, though I should add (not just for Mark and Alison, I mean for everyone who's jumping to the wrong conclusion right now) that the only thing going on in that bedroom was a night of cuddling. What was meant to be one night turned into a whole weekend together, and we've been together ever since. Together is a relative term in a long-distance relationship where you both travel extensively, but we've made it work. No relationship is ever smooth sailing, and we're just proud that we've managed to navigate our way through some tough times together and become stronger as a result.

Having Aimee with me during lockdown has also helped me stay positive. There's been so much bad stuff in all of it, but it's been absolutely amazing to spend such a huge amount of time together rather than just passing like ships in the night. I think it's particularly important to keep positive because without a strong mind and focus, receiving the news of lockdown and national restrictions could be career destroying for us. We had to think outside of the box to see what we were going to do moving forward. Being creative types, we both knew that it was possible - but how long for?

Episode 2 - What Now?

It hadn't officially been announced by Boris yet, but we could all tell which way the wind was blowing. Lockdown was clearly coming and I needed to make a plan of action, as opposed to burying my head in the sand.

I was on my way to Darlaston Town Hall, which ended up being my last live gig, to do a show with Bobby Davro - who has become a really good mate of mine. Bobby got in touch with me via Twitter after he saw me on 'Britain's Got Talent' back in 2015.

Hang on a second – you were on BGT? Yeah, it was 2015 and I got to the final and came 7th. That was one of the more stressful times of my life. It all started when I was doing a comedy club in Islington called the 'Hen and Chickens' and BGT producers had dropped in, scouting for talent they could put on TV. The day after the gig I received a phone call from one of the runners, asking me if I wanted to be up in front of the judges in Manchester. That's only two and a half hours from where I live in Hartlepool, so I thought why not? I agreed and he gave me all the details of when I would do my first audition.

Television's all about the details, so I had another phone call from a producer wanting to know everything: what impressions I was going to do, which material I was choosing, and everything else. It seemed a bit strange from the outside: I'd previously been under the impression that people just turned up, did their thing, and the judges then decided whether the act goes through or not. I was a bit taken aback when the producers started picking around at my act, trying to add stuff in and take stuff out. I wasn't completely sure how to respond.

My agent at the time was Anne George. She was looking over all of this and give me the best advice: "Do what you are comfortable with, remember this is going to be seen by millions of people and you know what works. You have tried it and tested it in the clubs and venues that I have sent you to, don't let them pressure you into doing anything you don't want to do. Once you're on that stage they have no control, remember that".

Anne was a very firm but very fair businesswoman. She knew her showbiz and exactly how these people operated. She was determined to get the very best for her acts, and she wasn't prepared to pull any punches at all. A couple of weeks later I had a phone call from yet another producer. Just how many producers does one show have, I wondered? This particular producer was asking me if I could change my audition from Manchester to Edinburgh.

I got halfway through my sentence, with "I've already got Manchester in the dia......" before they interrupted with an offer to pay for my flights and hotel. Having my expenses covered would be nice, but I also interpreted it as a bit of a show of confidence. They wouldn't be doing that if they didn't want me on television, so I thought it was a pretty good sign that they were intending to put me through to the next round. All I need to do, I thought, is do what they say and I'll be competing in the final in no time.

I called Anne to tell her the good news, but she was a little more down-to-earth about it. She didn't want me to get my hopes up too much, just in case it turned out not to be quite so perfect. Firstly, she told me, they should have called her first. Secondly, remember that when they pay for hotels and flights it's all tax-deductible. Take the expenses with a bit of a pinch of salt. It was good advice, but as it happens I needn't have worried. She finished with a little pep talk: if they want me to do Edinburgh, then I should go there and smash it out of the park – doing an act I know and feel comfortable with.

I flew in to Edinburgh Airport the day before my audition. It was an exciting time, but I'd learned from Anne that I needed to keep myself on my toes with these people and make sure that I don't get manipulated by them. There are some acts who've made a very good living out of the circuit for years, but by going on the show they've been ruined. I was going into this with my eyes wide open, taking that into consideration.

The venue was the Edinburgh Festival Theatre, and they'd set us up a waiting room in a large lobby area which would normally be used as a bar. There were tables and chairs scattered around, all of the acts nervously hanging around and chatting a bit whilst waiting. Everything you do in these situations is for the benefit of the television company, so there's plenty of waiting around.

We weren't called to stage straight away, but instead we were called in to talk to producers in another room. When my turn came, I was put in front of a camera and asked to spill some emotional beans about how I was feeling leading up to my audition. They asked some quite intrusive questions about my personal life which I wasn't willing to answer. It's quite troubling just how much stuff these people were able to find out about me. He seemed to think I was giving him a bit of a hard time, but I remembered what Anne said. We were both playing a game, and I was very aware that anything I said could be edited later. It was a great learning curve for me on how to deal with any form of media. They're so good at twisting things and they can ruin you if you let them.

One example of this as when the Daily Star called me up and asked me about life on the road one of the questions. They ask me whether I sleep in my car when I'm on a long drive. From my response "Of course if I am tired, I pull over and have a couple of hours sleep as it is not safe to drive tired", they somehow managed to print a little article the next day saying that I was homeless. They'll exaggerate anything to sell more papers.

They kept asking questions about my personal life, and I kept steering away from those and responding by talking about myself and my career. The interview dragged on. It took two hours of me talking in front of the camera: they kept interrogating me, no doubt hoping that I would break or slip and make a mistake. For every minute of television that's actually aired, there will be many times more material which will end up on the cutting-room floor. Anything you say can be taken out of context and used against you if you let it.

By the time we were finally done, it was around 3 o'clock and I was hanging around again. Given that the show wasn't going to start till 8pm, I thought to myself fuck this – and sneaked out of one of the side doors to head out to the nearest pub. It was a lovely little boozer with a nice landlord and it just had a relaxing vibe about it, which was exactly what I needed. The atmosphere back at the theatre was very tense. Everyone understandably looked so nervous and anxious. It was a big day for all of us, and we all had a lot riding on it, so sitting in that environment for hours before one of the most nerve-wrenching moments of your life wasn't exactly a good idea for anyone.

I only had a couple of glasses of wine and had water in between each glass to make sure I didn't over-egg the pudding. I knew the show was going to be on at 8pm, so I made sure that I got back to the theatre at 7pm and no one had even seemed to notice I had gone. After a little more waiting in the foyer area at around 9pm, it was finally my time to shine.

I was guided backstage by one of the runners and the sound guy gave me a microphone. A few paces closer to the wing and I was greeted by Ant and Dec. They were everything you can imagine them to be: just really lovely people, giving me a bit of reassurance and putting me at ease.

I walked out onto the stage in front of the judges. Everything happens so suddenly, and there'

It was just so surreal, I'm normally watching stuff like this from my sofa on my TV at home, but now it felt like I was inside my TV. My heart was racing and my mouth was going dry I needed water but it was too late, Simon had already spoken to me.

Simon: "How are you?"

Me: "I'm good Simon, how are you?"

Simon: "I'm good, what's your name please?"

Me: "Danny Posthill"

Amanda: *"Oh, that sounds like a pop star's name"*

Simon: *"Is that what you're going to do for us today?"*

Me: *"No, I'm going to do some impressions for you"*

Simon: *"Is this what you do for a living?"*

Me: *"Yeah, I do the comedy clubs, after dinners, anywhere that will pay me"*

Simon: *"So what would be more important then - doing the royal variety or winning the money?"*

Me: *"Well the money because I want to buy a house!"*

That got a laugh from the audience. Simon then went on to say "Well I was actually on the last Royal Variety performance" David then cut him off and said "Simon, you said 7 words and introduced last year's winners. That is not performing at the Royal Variety performance, I hosted it, now that's what you call performing at the Royal Variety - not saying 7 words."

The audience laughed with an applause break and I laughed too. Simon didn't seem to like it, with an atmosphere in the air that felt like the boss had been made a fool out of. Simon then cut it off and said to me "Well Danny, best of luck"

As I started my mouth was getting drier. There's something about having cameras on you and knowing there will be millions of people watching that makes you feel like someone's ramming a sock down your throat to stop you speaking.

I started with Billy Connolly and it got a titter. I moved onto John Bishop, getting a laugh. I moved through the gears with Gary Barlow, who really got them. Then I transitioned from David Beckham into Michael McIntyre and by this time the audience were rolling in the aisles. I had them in the palm of my hand.

As I was doing Michael McIntyre, I reminded Simon that Michael also hosted the Royal Variety performance and didn't say just seven words to introduce the previous year's winner. Unscripted comedy is often the best, because it absolutely set the place alive. The room was going crazy. Except for Simon – he just didn't like the fact that a working-class lad from Hartlepool had the room in the palm of his hand, or that he was still the butt of the joke from David's original comedy. I returned to Billy Connolly to say goodnight to the audience, getting a standing ovation. It felt amazing, a theatre of 2,000 people all standing up and applauding what I had done was just truly incredible. Words can't describe how good it felt. Attention then turned to the judges who all said that they thought it was brilliant, until we got to Simon who said "Well it was okay".

The audience then began to boo him which got his back up

even more. He then continued :

Simon: *"Well I didn't think your Beckham was very good and I think anyone can do him"*

Me: *"Well if anyone can do him why don't you give it a go".*

Everyone laughed and you could see he was getting angrier and to top it off the audience started chanting "Do it, Do it, Do it, Do it"

To be fair to Simon, he had a point. Looking back now it probably wasn't my best impression, but this could end up on TV so I couldn't back down. I thought if they show this on the telly I'll come over as a hero, an act that stood up to Simon Cowell the most powerful man in showbusiness. He then asked me, before Amanda butted in:

Simon: *"Why did you do Billy Connolly?*

Amanda: *"because we're in Scotland, Simon".*

Me: *"Thank you Amanda. Because we're in Scotland, Simon".*

You could see that he was seething. There's always a bit of a bite back with Simon, so I certainly wasn't going to escape it after

I'd just taken the piss out of him on stage. He concluded with "Well it's a bit passee, I've seen that a lot, but the reason you got a good reaction is because you're funny and people like you. But if you want to do well in this competition, you have to raise the bar and I don't think the bar was as high as it should be. David, yes or no?"

At this point I was questioning to myself whether I was going to get through or not. It's that moment, when you've done everything you can, and have to wait for the outcome – a bit like after sitting an exam at school. Fortunately it wasn't a long wait as all four of them gave a 'yes'. I was delighted to have made it through to the next stage. The back and forth with Simon was all cut when it went out on air. I guess Simon really didn't want that broadcast. That's the thing with TV though: you really have no control over which bits of a pre-record are actually going to be used.

Episode 3 -
Britain's Got Talent

Leading up to the semi-finals I was invited to a press day where the BGT lawyers were going to go through the contract with us and we were to sign the agreement. My agent Anne, always looking out for me, said "Don't go. They can send it and we will get our lawyers to look over the contract"

I can't really go into it all for legal reasons, but let's just say it didn't meet our requirements. Anne was going back and forth with producers saying that I wasn't going on the show unless we have it our way. After all the back and forth we eventually came to an agreement and I was going to be performing in the semi-final which was being recorded at the Fountain studios at Wembley.

Like the first audition, there was a lot of hanging around and the atmosphere was pretty tense. I went to sneak out of the studios before the show to have a quick beer to take the edge off it all, but I had to bypass security which made it a little trickier than the time before. I eventually managed to sneak out and found a bar round the corner. As I walked into the bar it was packed.

My first thought was this is the audience that's coming to see the semi-final, then all of a sudden it went so quiet - the type of silence you would witness when you walk into a local hardware store. I could hear my own footsteps as I walked to the bar and ordered my drink, with everyone looking at me. I thought that they must have all recognised me from my first audition on television. As I ordered my beer, two women were debating whether or not they should talk to me. I could see it all happening, feeling like a right Billy Big Bananas at this point. One of them eventually came over to me to talk.

"Excuse me", she said, and I turned to look at her. "Hello, you alright?", I replied. "This is a private party, could you please leave?" It brought me crashing right back down to earth. In hindsight, that's exactly what I needed at this point. When you're in a TV studio it's just not reality. You're accompanied everywhere you go, being given refreshments, having expenses paid for and assistance generally at hand if you need anything. It's like you're living in a different world, and this woman brought me right back down to earth - putting me in my place without even realising it. I was actually pretty grateful for that. I went next door to another bar, had a beer, and was back in the studio ready to go an hour before the show.

The producers were going through ideas leading up to the semi-final. Fortunately I'd saved some voices for the semi-final which the producers had originally wanted me to use in my first audition. That's the thing when you go into a show like this: you have to have a strategy and not burn yourself out on your first audition. You need to do just enough to get through, keeping some of your best material in reserve for the later stages. Anne had been proven absolutely right and the plan was working. To be fair to the producers they were really helpful and helped me to mould my set. I appreciate that they had experience in TV and particularly within BGT, but I had the first-hand experience with the audiences I had performed for over the years.

I wanted to do different characters at each stage of the competition, so I made sure I was doing different impersonations in the semi-final to the ones I'd done in my first audition. The only voice I repeated was Michael McIntyre but that was just to get me on, and I felt I had to do it as it went so well in my first audition. This time I included a Jimmy Carr impression. I wasn't sure whether one of the jokes would land, because it was specifically written to do on the show. It wouldn't work anywhere else, so I didn't have the option of testing it in front of an audience first. In the voice of Jimmy Carr I said:

"Last time I was on Britain's Got Talent it was fantastic. David said fantastic, Amanda said fantastic, and Alesha said fantastic. Simon said…put your hands on your head."

Luckily it got a big laugh and a round of applause. After that I switched to Alan Carr, which to be fair I didn't think was the best impression I've ever done of him. Watching it back later, I feel like I was shouting and that overpowered the impression. Perhaps this was because I was in such a large venue and I was fighting it rather than relaxing into it and letting the mic do the work. I then went into Sarah Millican which was a big success, before finishing on Ant and Dec which absolutely brought the place down. Ant and Dec also played along with it brilliantly and took it really well. It's a big risk impersonating people who are in the same room, but this paid off massively.

During the judges' comments they were all great but Simon had a little dig at me. I'd been expecting that after the first audition, no matter how good my set was. He said "I felt like you were losing the audience at one point". As the audience started to boo, he continued "but when you done the guys that's what saved you to be honest". I wondered whether that comment would have cost me, stopping me from making it through to the final. It was a hell of a line-up, so I was pleased to come runner-up and make it through to the final. I was absolutely over the moon. I came second to an incredibly talented singer Callum Scott, who is now a global superstar and has signed with Capital - who are a huge record label.

Me and Callum occasionally keep in touch and he is a lovely guy. Not long after BGT, me and Callum were invited to an MMA (Mixed martial arts) event in Birmingham. He was meant to be sitting next to us in the VIP area but there were other people sitting in Callum's seats. I saw Callum across the other side of the cage and he didn't know where he was supposed to be sitting. I directed him across and kindly told these other people that they were sitting in Callum and his family's seats. They didn't argue with me. They kindly moved, with Callum and his family sitting next to me and my friend John Dawson. John is a very good friend of mine and you will find out a lot more about him later on in the book.

After these other people moved, John explained to me that the people I'd just asked to move were the family of former world heavyweight boxing champion David Haye and that 'he wasn't happy about the whole thing and wanted a word with me'. It turned out that John was just messing with me but I'm not going to lie I was shitting myself up until I realised that he was winding me up. David Haye happened to be on the commentary that night and he looks as big in real life as he does on TV.

Leading up to the final, I only had two days to prepare. Luckily, I already had an idea of what I was going to do. I filmed it and sent it to the producers, and they pulled it to bits. I'd planned on doing a routine as if I was hosting "Take Me Out" as Paddy McGuinness. I planned to have a load of girls behind me with podiums like they have on the show. I was then going to introduce Simon and say "Hi my name's Simon and I'm from London". As Paddy would say, I'd ask "Girls are you turned on or turned off?" and then have all the girls buzz Simon off.

Unfortunately I couldn't get Simon's voice quite right as I couldn't go deep enough. They also didn't want to spend quite

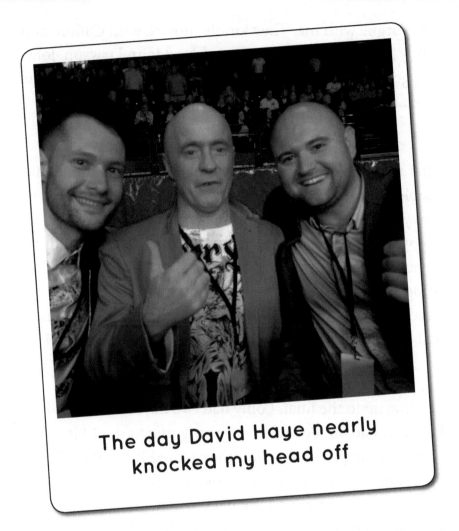

The day David Haye nearly knocked my head off

so much money on the production of something which would only be a short sketch. They also weren't too keen on the other voices I'd planned because they were concerned that the celebrities I was impersonating weren't famous enough. I told them to leave it with me.

By the next day I had managed to get a routine together which I didn't particularly feel comfortable with. I remembered the advice my agent Anne had given - not to do anything I'm uncomfortable with - so it was back to the drawing board. Before I knew it, it was the day of the final and I didn't have any material planned. I did have an idea, but not a solid plan. It left me with a massive headache, so bad that I couldn't get out of bed. At this point I was still staying in the hotel close by to the studio, which was all paid for by BGT. I called my producer Alan and he came to see me in my hotel room to check if I was okay. I was in so much pain that I wasn't sure whether I would be able to do the show or not.

Along with the uncertainty around the material I was doing, I think the stress of performing to 10 million people live on a Sunday night must have also brought it on. If anyone has had a migraine before you would know what it's like: a feeling that you can't lift your head off the pillow, and looking into the light is excruciating. This was the first time I'd ever had anything like a migraine, so it really wasn't helping.

Alan came back a couple of hours later, and given that I was still in the same condition they'd got another act on standby ready to fill my slot if needed. Shortly after Alan had gone, I got a phone call from Anne. She told me that they called her and said that I was watching TV and that I was faking it because I didn't have a set prepared.

I immediately thought 'the lying, cheeky bastards', but I was too ill to get angry. As I'm looking back, writing this, it's making me madder by the sentence: how dare they say that I was lying? Half an hour later, a doctor came to look at me and gave me some tablets. I asked her for extra painkillers to get me through it and she happily obliged. Soon after, Aimee then came into my hotel room along with Miles Crawford, a friend of mine. He basically said to me 'Dan, you're just going to have to try and get through it. Have a couple more painkillers and you'll be fine'.

I was still in two minds, but Aimee reminded me that this is a once in a lifetime opportunity. She said that I really have to do it now: I needed to get out of bed and pull myself together. By this point I was on co-codamol, paracetamol and something else beginning with 'e'. I can't remember what it was, but it certainly wasn't ecstasy. The painkillers started to work. I was beginning to shape up and feel a little better, so I agreed to perform. I had to take a stand on what material I was doing in order to get me through it with confidence and a clear head.

The producer said to me that he'd told me not to do these impressions because they're not famous enough. I knew that this was something I was confident doing, so I insisted: "Look, the show is in 2 hours. I'm going to tell you what impressions I'm doing and that's that." He then stormed off, and in a way I'm glad he did because I was getting so angry. I was just starting to feel better and wanted to get my head in the zone. I put a routine together which opened with Paddy McGuinness. From there I would go into Keith Lemon, then Johnny Vegas, Dara O'Briain, Lee Evans and Ant and Dec. The main issues the producer had were with Johnny Vegas and Dara O'Briain, but I was comfortable with the material I'd prepared for them and so it would have to do.

In the end it went really well, and I was already so proud of myself for getting that far. More than anything, I was just so relieved that I felt well enough to do it. Doctor Showbiz kicked in, along with all the other medication that was pumped into me. I finished seventh and I couldn't have been happier. I do think that the final might have taken a few years off my life with the stress of it all, but it has helped my career massively.

Episode 4 -
The Last Gig

It was my last gig before the first lockdown. Bobby had been impressed by my performances on BGT, so as you can imagine I'd felt pretty flattered. I used to watch Bobby on the TV when I was a kid, just like I think a lot of people did at the time. To us, he was Mr Saturday Night.

From the moment he got in touch, Bobby and I became great friends. He is kind enough to let me stay at his house when I have gigs down his way, and when I do, we always have a few drinks in his kitchen and do impressions till about 4 in the morning.

Bobby is a craftsman. A lot of people don't like to go on after him at a gig as he is a hard man to follow. He has torn the roof off of every place I have ever seen him work; he's an all-round entertainer, not just an impressionist, and there's not many of them around these days.

One night at his house, after a couple of drinks, Bobby came up with an idea. He would do a voice that I do, then I would top it, he would do another impression then I would top that. This then became a routine, and it all developed into me being his 'impressionist coach'. Bobby is very generous in the way that he doesn't mind giving other people the limelight. He lets them get laughs, and there's not many performers like that. A lot of us can be very needy and don't like to give credit where credit is due. During the act he would slowly pretend to get pissed off because I was outdoing him. He would do his impression and I would top all of them. To be fair, they were all voices in my repertoire that were not in his. It's such a great example of him being a generous performer, feeding me the laughs, almost at his own expense, and letting it happen.

Of course it's all endearing on his part, gets the audience on both our sides for different reasons, and creates a successful routine. To top it all off he would say, "Who else do you do then?", and I would do an impression of him and he would kick me off the stage. It got a huge round of applause and Bobby came up with the whole thing.

If I had a night off and was staying at his house and he had a gig, I would go to the gig with him, and he would get me up and we would do this routine to a huge applause. It got better and better every time to the point where me and Bobby started doing shows together. We had a couple of dates booked in for 2020, but unfortunately, they all got pulled. That was such a shame because it was something different as opposed to just going out on the road on your own.

Besides the impressionist coach routine, we would also tell a story about when we met Billy Connolly, which I have to say is one of the most memorable moments of my life. My other half

Aimee knows how much I adore Billy, so she got me tickets to go and see him in his last ever tour at the Hammersmith Apollo. She couldn't come with me, so I asked Bobby to come along, which turned out to be a be a blessing. A few years ago, Billy sadly got diagnosed with Parkinson's disease, which no doubt had (or at least will have) an impact on his career and ability to work.

So we were sat in our seats, ready for the show to start, and Billy slowly walked out onto the stage. As he walked on, the audience gave him a standing ovation. Rightly so, because the man is a legend. The audience eventually sat down and got settled, then Billy said in the most beautifully timed way,

"You only done that because I'm ill."

The laughter erupted and the applause started again. It must have lasted for over a minute, it was incredible. Billy did 1 hour and 40 minutes, and it was a masterclass in stand-up comedy. Not only were my sides aching from laughter, but I was just amazed at how good he was! Bobby knew how much I loved Billy, and could see how much I had enjoyed the show, so he then said to me,

"Come on, were going to go and meet him."

At this point I thought Bobby was winding me up, as he is good at that. He does things such as putting a spoon through a coffee cup handle at the dinner table, and then pretends to spill the cup over you, but the spoon stops the cup from falling off the saucer. Or when you reverse your car and he's in the passenger seat, he will hit the door with his hand so you think you have crashed your car into something. Bobby being Bobby, I was prepared for a wind up, so I said:

"How do you know Billy?"

"You'll see, come on follow me."

So off we went, and at this point I was still sure he was winding me up. We got to the security guards who were at the stage door. The conversation between Bobby and the security guy went something like this:

"Is there any chance we can go and see Billy? Its Bobby Davro."

"Don't know who you are mate, have you got a pass?"

"No, I don't. But could you please let backstage know that Bobby Davro is here and he would like to see Billy."

The security guy speaks into his radio.

"There's a guy here, Bobby Davro, says he knows Billy or something?"

Me and Bobby were stood there waiting whilst this guy was looking at us with an attitude. You could see he was hoping that we were not going to get backstage. I'm not saying that this guy was a jobsworth, because at the end of the day he did have to do his job, and make sure that the artists and crew were safe. I get that, but there's a certain way of doing things and his attitude didn't really sit right with me. Eventually there was a reply.

"Send them through"

We got in! I'm backstage and I am going to get to meet *the Billy Connolly*, but all the while I was still wondering how Bobby knew Billy. And when had they met before? So, I kept asking Bobby:

"How do you know Billy?

Bobby was just replying "you'll see, you'll see". By this point we were outside of Billy's dressing room and Bobby was talking to this guy who he seemed to know quite well. I politely introduced myself to him, then off he went, I asked Bobby "Who was that?"

He said "Oh, Elton John's road manager." Of course, it was, I mean we were backstage at a Billy Connolly gig. It's not going to be Ron from a working men's club, who is telling you that you're going on after the pigeon racing results, which is something I have got pretty used to over the years. To me backstage is sitting in a green room, with a few comics, having a moan about the traffic or the trains on the way there. To be fair I do love catching up with other comics before a gig. I adore the circuit, but you get where I am coming from, this is backstage at a gig of a superstar who is loved dearly by millions, so you can expect it to be a little different.

The door opens, and there he is: the comedy shrine that is Sir Billy Connolly. He had such a presence about him, and you can see why people call him the Big Yin. As we walked into his dressing room, I sort of froze, my heart was beating so fast, I was shaking. As we walked in Billy done the point that he does, he pointed at Bobby and he said "Bobby Davro, the bravest man I know."

I thought this is interesting, how is Bobby brave? I can't wait to hear this! Billy continued, "The only man who was brave enough to sit next to Salman Rushdie in a restaurant, and is still alive." Now I didn't really know who Salman Rushdie was, until Bobby told me after. For those of you who don't know, he is a novelist who wrote a very controversial book called "The Satanic Verses". He was getting a lot of stick for it at the time, and that's why people were afraid to sit near him.

Me and Billy

So anyway, why is Bobby brave? There was a party back in the day which was attended by a few celebrities, and this was where Billy saw Bobby sat next to Salman Rushdie. It turned out the reason Bobby sat next to Mr Rushdie was because he had 4 empty seats next to him, and Bobby felt sorry for him, but at the time Bobby didn't know how controversial he was. That's the kind of guy Bobby is, he doesn't like to see people feeling left out or alone.

They were sat in the dressing room laughing about this, and then Bobby kindly introduced me to Billy and said,

"This is my good friend Danny Posthill, he's a great impressionist."

Billy then looked right at me, and said thoughtfully some words that I'll never forget:

"Do you know, that's something I have always wanted to be able to do."

I was speechless for a short while, it was only a few seconds, but it seemed like an eternity. I then snapped out of it and I started to tell Billy how much I adore his work, and that whenever I have a down day, I watch his cardinals school visit joke on YouTube, as it makes me laugh every time. Which Billy replied to me with,

"The thought of it though is funny in itself, a cardinal telling a wee boy to fuck off." Me and Bobby laughed, and then we said our goodbyes.

To say that I was on Cloud Nine is an understatement. Me and Bobby talk about this day on a regular basis, and as I said before, this little story has now made its way into our show.

Of course, we add a few bits in for comedic effect. We talk about me having done an impression of Billy to Billy. That never happened, because I was too nervous and I don't think he would have liked that anyway. In fact, we told the story at the last gig we did in Darlaston Town Hall.

We finished the gig on such a high, and then we sat in the dressing room wondering what was going to happen next now that Coronavirus had hit the UK.

On my way home from the gig, I was in the car and talking to Aimee on the phone (via the hands-free obviously) and I was talking about what to do next. I came up with an idea of doing personalised voice recordings for people's birthdays, or doing a gig online and selling tickets. It wouldn't be the same, but could at least get us by financially, as we didn't know how long this pandemic was going to last.

Within a couple of days, the announcement was made that we were going into a full national lockdown. All I could do now was think positive, do what I could regarding work, trying to get some business online, and make the best of a bad situation.

On the other hand, it's all very well having good intentions and having a positive mindset, but is this going to earn money, put food on the table and pay the bills?

This was going to be tough!

Episode 5 -
Earning A Crust

I am the type of person who doesn't dwell on things. I just get on with it. A couple of years ago I learned this because I realised I was too hesitant with many things, and it sometimes lost me opportunities. As soon as the pandemic came along, I had no choice.

I looked over the ideas that I had with the video messages and the online gig. I looked on the internet to see if I could do a private link via Facebook or YouTube but I couldn't seem to find a way. To be fair I've never really been that good with technology. Well I say that, but I think it's partly just laziness. It's like when you see some people of the older generation asking you about Facebook, they are keen to get on it because the rest of their family are on there, but when you go to show them, they say,

"Oh, that's too complicated for me, I can't be bothered with all that"

My Nana is the best. She said to me,

"I've seen that video when you were taking off Diane Abbott, went well on Twitter the other day"

(Taking off I know)

I said, "Nana you're not on Twitter?"

She said "Oh no, I watched it via Google. I don't sign up to Twitter just in case they get my bank details."

Nanas will always bring humour to your life, especially my Nana. The best one was when she was putting her wheely bin out and her neighbour from over the road said to her "Pauline, do you get the Sun?"

My Nana replied with "Well on a morning we get it out the back, and on the afternoon we get it out the front." Priceless!

I remember talking to Tom Eaves, who I know via my cousin Tony Hamilton because they are both professional jockeys. Tom told me a story about his Nana, which I thought was an absolute belter, he said he went round her house one day and she seemed to be in a bit of a mood with him. The conversation went something like this:

Tom: *"Everything ok Nana?*

His Nana: *"No"*

Tom: *"Why?"*

His Nana: *"Well I tried to call you the other day and you ignored me, and some woman answered your phone!"*

Tom: *"Nana, no one else answers my phone, and plus I'm not even seeing anyone!"*

Nana: "Well you must be, because a woman definitely answered and she said 'she can't take your call right now', and you must have met her at some nightclub you've been going to called O2, because that's where she said she was from."

He then had to explain to her that it was his answerphone on his mobile, and his network provider was O2.

Anyway, I was looking into how I can earn money whilst staying at home, and I had to start looking into the logistics of doing gigs online. I soon found out about something called Zoom, which is like Skype, but you can have as many participants in the call as you want.

That was my Eureka moment. I could do a few Zoom gigs, a few personalised voice messages and I'm sorted. That will get me through, and my bank account won't get rinsed. So that very day I put a video out on my social media, explaining what I was going to do. I had quite of interest, however there was the odd comment saying that I was desperate, and if I wasn't a shit comedian I wouldn't have to resort to this. This is one of the other reasons I didn't really want to put content online, because of wankers like this.

I have always been a gigging comic doing the circuit, corporate events, holiday parks and clubs, and I put all of my time and effort into that because I would turn up and get a financial reward for making people laugh. Even if I did have a dickhead in the audience, I wouldn't really be that bothered, as I get paid and that's that. The small minority of idiots are forgotten about.

In the past I always felt that I didn't want to put myself through dealing with trolls by prostituting myself out online for no financial reward - what's the point? But as soon as the live gigs were gone, I needed to do these videos and put content online to make a living. I know trolls are a minority, but God can they piss you off!

There are times when I have been in a mood because of a comment someone made about me online, and it then puts Aimee in a mood because I'm in a mood, then I realised this is what these idiots want. I've got to the stage now where I just take it as part of the job and I don't let it get to me. It's similar to when I started doing stand-up.

I used to take hecklers really seriously, but now I just deal with them and move on. I also like to think if you start getting trolled it means you're doing well; you're in the limelight, these people have seen your videos and know who you are.

I know that deep down trolls have issues themselves. There are comedians who I don't particularly find funny, or musicians who aren't my cup of tea, but I wouldn't go out of my way to publicly slate them online. It's just unnecessary. To add to that, being an entertainer myself I respect how hard they have worked, and even though what they do might not be to my taste, there will be people out there who love them. The more I have been sharing online work, the more I have been exposed to trolls, and the more I actually feel sorry for them.

Yes, that's right. I feel sorry for these people who are saying nasty things. If I was sat on my own, at my laptop, with no-one around me, no friends or family and hated everything about my life, then maybe I would think the same way as these trolls. It's sad, and I wish they would get out and start living - instead of existing through a keyboard, getting some sort of satisfaction from writing hurtful comments. This is the problem with social media. As amazing as it is for certain things, it also gives too many people a platform to speak, and that's when it can get out of control, and lead people, not just celebrities, down a dark path if they are being bullied online.

Then you get the other types, the self-righteous opinionated people, who like to get the moral high ground on whatever you put online. These people like to think that their opinion is highly valued, and that everyone else is beneath them. I have had a few run-ins of this kind, mainly from when I posted an impression of Diane Abbott. Many people who enjoy my work say that this is my best impression, and people request this specific one quite a lot. However, I have had comments regarding this impression from the self-righteous crowd calling me a racist, which I find laughable.

When I do an impression of Diane Abbott, I make no reference to the colour of her skin. Nor do I 'black up'. I make reference to the fact that she has said some dumb shit over the years, and whenever she is in the news, she continues to say dumb shit. As an impressionist I am going to capitalise on this impression, as it is current and relevant to today, and I am going to continue with it, especially if my audience enjoys watching this particular impersonation. When people try to call me a racist for the impression, the conversation generally goes like this:

Self-righteous troll: "RACIST!"

Me: "Racist? How?"

Self-righteous troll: "White man impersonating a black woman, I think you'll find that is racist."

Me: "Ah right, so you think as a white man I shouldn't impersonate someone who is a different colour to me, as that is offensive, and it makes me a racist?"

Self-Righteous Troll: "Yes. Stop doing it!"

Me: "Ok, so you don't think I should impersonate people who are a different colour to me, I should not include them in my act, I should not present a multicultural society within my act, which is what this country is, and so I should only impersonate people who are white?"

That's when they start to backtrack, and say something like:

Self-righteous troll: "You can't explain things like this to racist idiots like you."

Me: "You haven't answered my question. You don't think I should be inclusive to all cultures and races, and I shouldn't impersonate people that have different colour skin to me?

Occasionally you get the ones who respond with "Yes" – to which I reply "Well if that's the case, then you're the racist!"

I don't even bother to respond to people now, as my mate Dave (the more intelligent one who proofread this book for me) just deals with them. I think he quite enjoys it, and I'm grateful as I can just sit back and 'like' his replies. To be fair I do find it so much funnier watching the self-righteous people getting really angry and frustrated when Dave ties them in knots, I mean most of the time they tie themselves in knots. Its best to just let people get on with their life, you get on with yours, and we will all have a good day.

I am not going to bow down to a minority of people who just want to silence you, all because they don't agree with it. I remember Ricky Gervais came up with the perfect line, "If I had a pound for everyone who I have offended...oh actually I have", and I think good for him. Comedy is comedy, and the more people who follow the lead of Ricky Gervais the better.

My Diane Abbott impression has also led me onto further opportunities. Alex Belfield has invited me onto his YouTube Channel a number of times doing not just Diane Abbott, but Trump and Ben Shapiro, so I am not going to let the offended police silence me online when I know that it can generate other work. It's complete nonsense. Alex Belfield was originally a reviewer, and a very well-respected one at that. He reviewed shows all over the world, including one of the places I love, Las Vegas. Most performers feared him because he spoke the truth, and people don't always like the truth, but now he puts that into practice talking about the world today, daily news and current affairs, which has proved very popular.

His YouTube channel is growing like wildfire, with over 225,000 subscribers and still counting, so for him to invite me onto his show was really flattering. Anyway, after I put out the video promoting my online ideas to try and make myself a bit of money, I got loads of interest with the personal video messages.

I was recording about 15 to 20 videos a day, and some of them were from the same customers. I would sit all day in the office doing personalised messages for people, thinking to myself I could get used to this. It was great: each day I would wake up and have the convenience of working and making money from home. People gave me great feedback each time, saying that I have made their son's birthday, or I have made their wife smile as she has been having a hard time lately. It was nice to know I was spreading a little joy, and having a positive impact.

Episode 6 - Comedy Online

A few days after doing the Diane Abbott impressions, I got a message from a social media brand called "The Hook", who have a huge social media following. They asked to have a meeting with me via Zoom. I thought okay, let's see what all this is about. We went through a few ideas of different videos we could create online, and ended up settling on a series of sketches, called 'Celebs in Lockdown'.

I do remember (how could I forget?) that at one point, about halfway through the meeting, I had to go to the toilet and it was pretty urgent! Have you ever been in a situation where you just need to go for a poo, and there is absolutely no warning - you just need to go? A friend of mine Stephanie Aird, a very funny comedian who has a huge following on Facebook, calls it "being a slave to your arse". She is bang on with that figure of speech.

One of the guys was talking about an idea, and I just said, which sounded quite abrupt, but I simply had no choice, "Guys I need to stop you there, and I need to come back on the call in a couple of minutes". To them it could have meant anything. I was trying to be discreet, but more than likely they probably just thought I was a rude bastard. To be fair it was my first time meeting them, so I didn't really want to say to them "two minutes lads, I need a shit". It's not something that you do. It's like when you meet someone for the first time and you slip a fart out thinking, "I'll get away with this", then you smell it knowing it's an absolute barn-burner, so you slowly start to back off from them. So I went for my poo, came back two minutes later, and got on with it. Luckily they didn't ask me where or why I had gone, I didn't say what I had done, and it was just back to business.

There was no money involved in this project, but I knew they had a large following, and it could help for me to get my followers up, and in turn sell more personalised messages. The way the guys edited the video and put it together was brilliant. It was imaginative and very well animated too. (If you want to check it out its on my YouTube channel @DannyPosthillComedian). The first one went out and it was very well received, so they wanted to make some more, in the meantime I was still doing the personalised messages for people and things were going great.

Alongside this I also managed to get a Zoom gig organised. Aimee created the poster (she is more technical than me) and we worked hard to sell tickets across social media. I was slightly worried about what the quality of the call would be like, and if there were going to be any technical hitches. I set everything up in my kitchen, and tried to run it like it was a proper gig; I had my suit on, with my laptop balanced on the chair, which itself was balanced on the table in front of me (so maybe not so normal, but the best I could do). Throughout the gig I had all the audience on mute, to save any interruptions and background noise, but I hadn't pre-empted that this would mean I hear no audience reaction or laughter myself. This was a bizarre feeling. I found it quite difficult to judge the audience and know when to move on. I would finish a gag and wait, then I would see laughter on the little screens in front of me. I was taken aback at first, as it looked like no one was laughing, but I soon realised it's because there was about a 5 second delay.

I finished the show and people loved it. The only complaints I had were from people who couldn't log in, though Aimee was frantically running around throughout trying to figure out Zoom and get people in the gig from her phone, to my phone, to the laptop! I think she found the whole experience more stressful than me, but we were more than happy to give these people a refund. At this time Zoom was a learning curve for all of us, as brand-new programme which had hardly been heard of. By now, I imagine almost every household is familiar with it.

The next two episodes of 'Celebs in Lockdown' went out online, which were also very well received, then all of a sudden... nothing! I didn't hear anything more from the guys from 'The Hook' (I don't think it was to do with the poo incident), and I came to the conclusion that the idea had run its course.

Clearly they didn't feel that they needed any more episodes. Looking on the plus side, I had some great content, and had gained some more online followers, as I had hoped would happen. I also got a phone call from my local newspaper, the Hartlepool Mail, who wanted to do an article about the videos. I thought that was quite a nice touch. By this point the personalised videos were also starting to slow down, and I was doing maybe one or two a day, which was a little disappointing but still better than nothing.

After a few days I started to get lazy, playing on my X-Box for most of the day, and wasn't even exercising. Luckily, that only lasted a few days. I received a message on my Facebook from a guy called Kane William Smith, who runs a Facebook page called Joke Pit. Kane wanted to have a chat with me, once again to discuss creating online content. I was so glad for this opportunity, and was happy that what I was already putting out there was creating interest. We had a meeting using a programme called Stream Yard, which I wasn't particularly familiar with, but he explained how everything worked and we soon started to have meetings back and forth about certain ideas. I then had a new project to focus my attention on, creating some extra new content which kept my brain fresh and creative, and to top it off, Kane had the skills and ability to edit my videos for me, making them look more professional and eye-catching.

Kane also got me involved in some online panel shows, which was another first for me. I ended up doing this every week, and I had so much fun. One of the shows was, "What gets my goat?", where we had 4 comedians plus a host, and we would basically talk about things that simply pissed us off. I had such a laugh doing that show, and it was also great that I got to meet comedians who I had never met before such as Dee Maxwell and Esther Minato, both very funny people.

Around this time, we also started up the "Phannie and Danny Sunday Sesh" with Stephanie Aird, who I mentioned earlier in the chapter. Steph is just nuts, and doesn't give a shit, a rebellious type of comedian who appeals to the everyday working-class person. She touches the hearts of real people, and that's why she is so loved by her online following, otherwise known as her "Phannies". The other interesting fact about Steph is that she used to be my technology teacher at secondary school. I used to do an impression of her in the classroom, and we reunited after I impersonated her online. We met up and have become great friends ever since.

Considering I was out of work, I was actually super-busy and my schedule hardly had a gap. another project I was working on was a show called 'Ted and Bozza's Late show'. I played the part of Boris Johnson, and another comic called Phil Smith played a character called Ted Hanky. Ted Hanky is an outrageous character who would ask me questions, and get everyone else who was watching to ask me questions too. To be fair they weren't political, just very filthy material. The whole show was improvised, which was great training for us to both think on our feet. To mix things up a bit, we also did a few shows where I played Donald Trump. Having Boris and (previously) Trump as the two world leaders has been absolute luxury for any impressionist who does topical material about political figures.

Being Trump

What I loved about all these panel shows was that they kept me busy, and kept me writing, because I had to. Doing different shows each night really kept me on my toes. I preferred living my lockdown life this way, as opposed to just waiting for it to end. In a way this was my comedy gym, getting me ready for when I go back to doing the real thing.

As much as I was being creative, by this point my income had massively dropped, and my personalised videos were coming in few and far between. I was now lucky if I was doing two a week, and I think it had just run its course. On the plus side I was still putting content online, which was very well received, particularly on Twitter. Twitter can be a funny one, as the maximum length video you can post is 2 minutes 20 seconds, so my sketches had to be within a certain time frame. Not only that, once it's out it's out, and you can't edit your tweet. If you put a video out and it starts to get loads of views, and there's a spelling mistake (which people like to point out), you can't edit it like you can on Facebook.

All in all, I am incredibly grateful for the internet, as it gives me somewhere to go to be creative. You don't always make money from videos posted on social media, unless you have millions of views. Regardless of there being no real financial gain, it was good for my mental health, and kept my creativity going. I am thankful for that.

Around June, like many people I did begin to question how long this lockdown was going to last. Originally, I expected it to be over in a couple of months. The longer it was going on, the more I could see that it would be a long wait before I could get back to performing live gigs. Before lockdown, I had a good income, and I was keen to get earning money again, but if my gigs weren't to come back anytime soon, I felt like it was time to try and think of another plan in order to make some money. Becoming homeless and losing everything I had worked hard for just wasn't an option.

Episode 7 - Get another job?

I started thinking to myself that I might need to get a 9 to 5 job, so I got in touch with a couple of mates who could get me some manual labour work just to tick me over until things got back to normal. The other question I was asking myself was 'what is normal? Is this the new normal?'

I had a chat with Aimee and she just said to me "look, we are okay for now, concentrate on putting more content on social media and do what you do best. You can go out and get a job, but if you do that you won't be fresh in people's minds when you do go back out gigging."

She had a point to be fair, I did say to her that I could work in the day and produce content on a night, she said "That's all well and good but you will be tired, and then probably just get home and play your X-Box. You haven't done a day job in years, and it's something you're not used to. Plus, we are not that desperate yet, so just hold off."

I have done loads of jobs over the years. The first job I ever had, like a lot of people when they were teenagers, was a paper round. I used to get £13 per week and sometimes I would work as a 'super spare', which meant if someone didn't turn up I would cover their paper round too. I remember I once covered another paper round and I couldn't find the right houses, so it got to the point where I had to go because I would be late for school. Anyway, I went to school as normal, and then went back home once school was finished, and as I got through the door my Mam was on the phone to someone screaming and shouting.

This isn't completely out of character for my mum, she is a feisty woman (in a good, caring way), but I couldn't for the life of me think who she would be talking to, and what on earth had happened. I stood in the doorway listening, and it soon clicked what the conversation was about, my Mam said "How dare you, he's a good boy, he is already doing one paper round, plus he's doing you a favour by doing an extra one, and he works hard, and don't forget he has school to go to as well. I don't think he would have missed 14 papers, that's ridiculous". As she was on the phone, I creeped upstairs and started playing on my PlayStation. I was half way through a career mode on WWF Warzone and my then my Mam shouted upstairs "DANIEL!"

When your mam or teacher calls you by your full Christian name you know you're in trouble. I shouted down "What?", pretending I didn't know what was going on, and I am her little goody two shoes who would never do anything wrong.

Mam: "How many papers have you missed?"

Me: "Only a couple."

Mam: "A couple as in 14? I've just been on the phone to the shop kicking off. And there seems to be 14 fresh newspapers in the dustbin outside, I don't remember buying 14 newspapers today and throwing them away!"

I knew I was in the wrong and clearly so did my Mam. I mean I could have been a little cleverer with the disposing of the evidence, but she didn't call the shop and apologise, which I was quite grateful for. I went to work the next day and not a word was said. The moral of the story is your Mam will always have your back no matter what, and to be fair it's not like it was a major crime at the end of the day. I had to be at school, and my education was more important.

She still hasn't apologised to the shop

I was non-stop at that age; I'm surprised I kept everything together. Mondays I would do my paper round, go to school, paper round after school, then I would have goalkeeper training. I played football for Hartlepool United youth team at the time, and all the goalkeepers would train on a Monday. Tuesdays I would do the same: paper round, school, paper round, then I would get the bus to Stockton (about 20 minutes away), do a judo lesson, and then Dave (my judo coach) would kindly drive me to another training session in Spennymoor. That was a hard class. I was 15 at the time and I would be training with men, some who were on the GB team and they were true technicians. I remember training with a couple of Iranian internationals, and they were as tough as they come, throwing me around with no remorse. I would take some bumps there, but at the end of the day they accepted me into the class, so they must have thought I could hack it. I used to finish the day absolutely shattered, and then have to get up the next day and do my paper round aching all over.

On Wednesday nights I would have football training with the first team, then I had 20 minutes to spare to get to Karate class. Thursdays again I would have first team training, then head off to an MMA (Mixed Martial Arts) class. There weren't many MMA gyms around then, and that used to be really tough. We would practice techniques for half an hour, then after that half an hour of sparring, and we didn't take it easy on each other either. It was like Fight Club. Fridays I would have nothing on, which to be fair I needed. I would be bruised and battered from all the training of the past week. My weekends were just as jam-packed, Saturdays I would play football for the district, and Sundays I would play football for Hartlepool.

To this day I still don't know where I got the energy from. My Mam used to say to me "you're doing too much, you're going to have a burnout", but I didn't care, I used to love it. I made so many friends, it was a great social life. Plus, now I'm older I can see that I benefited from having a busy schedule, as it meant I wasn't hanging around the streets causing trouble. It's given me the good work ethic I've got today. As well as that I used to pay for all my lessons with my paper round money, which made me feel like I had a bit of my own independence, and also set me up for adult life.

I quite enjoyed doing my paper round, but over time new opportunities came along. My Grandad got me a job as a glass collector on a Wednesday night at my local social club. I used to get 13 pounds a night. Technically I was too young to work there, but no one ever dared to argue with my Grandad, as he never backed down (this must be where my Mam gets it from). My Grandad wasn't just my Grandad, he was like my best mate. He used to love coming to watch me play football, he would come to every game. My uncle Paul used to say to me:

Paul: "Do you mind when my dad watches you play football?"

Me: "No, why?"

Paul: "I wouldn't tell him when I used to play, he used to shout from the sidelines and put me off."

Of course my uncle Paul loved his dad, but there's a certain time when you just like to get on with the game, and not have to worry about what the next thing would be to come out of my Grandad's mouth. I was different. I didn't really care. If I'm honest I used to quite like the drama, which is probably the reason I ended up in showbusiness. It did get to the point where there was a letter sent to all the players, telling parents to leave it to the managers when it comes to shouting advice on the pitch (though obviously worded a little nicer than that).

That weekend we were playing away at Halifax, and we lost the game by one goal. Normally I hate making excuses for a loss, but I think everyone who watched that game would agree. Let me explain, basically it was the referee's fault. How the hell that man got his badge to referee a game was beyond me. Fair play to my Grandad who held back and kept quiet, well at least until the end that was.

I was walking back to the changing room with the lads and all I heard was my Grandad's voice shouting across the field, "Here

Ref." I thought here we go, what's he going to say, he's going to get banned from watching me at this rate. My Grandad continued, "I'll give you marks out of 10, fucking 1 for turning up."

Me and the lads just fell about laughing, and to be fair so did some of the opposing team. They must have also noticed how bad he was even though they won. The next week at training not a word was said, and my Grandad carried on, not holding back, but no one could change that, so they stopped trying.

I used to love working in the Catholic club. When I had my little 5-minute break I used to sit with my Grandad and his mates, have a pint of coke and a bag of crisps, and listen to them put the world to rights. I used to always offer my crisps around the table. One time I asked my Grandad if he wanted a crisp and he took about ten. I then asked his mate Dave if he wanted one, now Dave was a big guy at the time. He's lost a lot of weight since, but back then he was enormous. If he walked past a TV you would have missed 3 episodes.

When I offered Dave a crisp he replied with "No thanks son I'm fine". Normally when someone who is overweight turns down food you don't say anything out of politeness, but my Grandad decided to pipe up.

My Grandad: "What was that Dave, you're turning down food? What's going on there?"

Dave: "I've got a belly ache."

My Grandad: "A belly ache? You must be in some pain you fat bastard."

People used to take the piss out of each other, and everyone still got on fine. That's what I loved back then. Now it seems as though everyone is just so easily offended, it's nice when you can have a joke and laugh without having to worry about the consequences. I mean maybe my Grandad was sometimes a little extreme, but he was a character, and people loved him for it.

After a couple more months my Grandad managed to get me extra shifts, so I was working weekends as well and I left my job as a paper boy. Out of all my shifts I used to love working weekends the most. Saturday was karaoke, so I would always look forward to getting up to sing. I remember someone on the committee had a little moan about it, and said that I should be working. In my defence, all the glasses were taken to the bar on time. This particular committee man had it in for me, and one night after I sang a song I came back down from the stage to collect the glasses, and he turned to me and said, "Here son, I would stick to your glass collecting if I was you."

I said "Here mate, I would stick to your drinking if I was you, I've been pissing in your lager for the past 3 weeks." I was obviously joking, but striving to be a comedian you take note from the greats, and they always seem to have that rebellious side. I was just following their lead. To be fair I've said worse to a policeman, and he had a gun. At the time I didn't know he had a gun, but Billy Big Bollox from the committee who had a bee in his bonnet over me singing a little bit of Westlife was no threat. He tried to report me for speaking to him like that, but I carried on with my glass collecting, and in the end they just used to let me sing.

Sunday nights we would have an act on. Sometimes it would be a comedian, which inspired me and led me further into comedy. One night we had a comedian on Called Chris McGlade, who absolutely tortured me during his set as I was walking around collecting the glasses. Not only did he torture me, but he tortured everyone. He was going behind the bar taking the crisps. "Who wants some crisps?", he would say, then start throwing the crisps out around the room. I couldn't believe it. The committee were seething, but no one stopped him because the audience were in tears of laughter. This bloke was outrageous, I had never seen anything like this before in my life and it really opened up my eyes of how to do comedy outside the box.

A few years later I was doing a comedy club, and he was also on the bill. I got talking to him and told him that he tortured me once when I was a glass collector in a club. It felt so surreal that we were now going to be performing on the same stage. Since then, me and Chris have become really good friends. He's such a talented comedian, but because his opinion doesn't fall in line with the establishment, he's unfortunately had the door closed on him by a few people. Being the determined man that he is, this hasn't stopped him going to the Edinburgh festival every year and getting rave reviews. I was in Edinburgh with him in 2019, and because it was my first time doing it, I was a little nervous and apprehensive. Chris reassured me before I started my run and simply said to me,

Chris: "You'll be alright here, Dan."

Me: "Why do you think that?"

Chris: "Because you're not shit."

I started laughing, but Chris was deadly serious, he said "No I'm serious Dan, you're not shit, so you'll be fine". That's Chris all over. Then he said, as he always does, "You're still a glass collector in my eyes though son" and we both laughed.

When I was glass collecting, I was still playing football and doing martial arts, so I still had a pretty hectic life. One night when I was at training, John Dawson who runs CCA (the MMA gym I go to) told me about a martial arts store that was opening up. Me and all the lads at the gym were buzzing. The opening day we were all there, first people in, looking around the shop. They sold pads, gloves, bags and even weapons. By this point I'd left school, so I wasn't playing football for my district any more. I used to train at the MMA gym on a Saturday and on my way there I would stop off at the shop and talk to Terry the manager.

Terry was a bubbly character from Leeds and had a very welcoming personality about him which is always a great trait to have when you own a shop. We would talk about martial arts for hours. One day I walked into the gym and John said to me, "By the way I was in the shop earlier on, just as you had left, and I said to Terry are you going to give my mate Danny a Saturday job or what? He comes in every day, he loves talking to the customers, why don't you give him a chance?"

Terry ended up giving me a job, and I used to work 2 hours on a Saturday before I went training. Sometimes he used to leave me there on my own. It was quite scary really, leaving me, a 16-year-old, in a shop on my own surrounded by Samurai swords. I never told my mam he used to leave me there on my own, nor did I tell her that they used to sell Samurai swords - she would have had a fit. I did love it there though, listening to people come into the shop and talk about where they train and what they do. People used to come from all over the North

East, because there weren't many shops like that around, and online shopping wasn't as accessible as it is today.

I've had a few jobs over the years. I used to do a bit of painting and decorating with my stepdad John, and I always had a laugh working with him. John can be really laid back which used to make it a better working environment and you still got stuff done, though I did stress him out sometimes. The problem of being a 'slave to my arse', as I mentioned in an earlier chapter, has been a problem all my life. I used to always need the toilet everywhere I went, in fact I still do, and it always happens at the most inconvenient times. In every house we worked in I had to have a shite, and in one house we were working on there was no door on the bathroom.

I was holding ladders for John in the hallway downstairs while he was painting the ceiling, when it hit me: I needed to go.

Me: "John, I need a shite"

John: "Oh Daniel man, you're a nightmare, can you not hold it in?

Me: "No I need to go; I'll be as quick as I can"

John: "There's no door on the bathroom, and the lady is going to be back soon, the last thing she wants to see is you having a shite in her house"

Me: "I'll be quick"

John: "Well hurry up!"

I ran upstairs to get on with my business. The toilet was just at the top of the landing, but as soon as I pulled my pants down and started to take a dump the lady came home. I could hear her at the front door, about to make her way up the stairs. Fair play to John, he kept her talking for 20 minutes until he heard the chain flush. He went down as a legend in my eyes that day. When I came back down and the woman had disappeared, he said:

John: "You told me you were going to be quick"

Me: "You know yourself John, you can never estimate how long its gonna take to come out"

John: "Did you spray the air freshener?

Me: "No"

Thankfully it didn't really smell, and the lady had one of those Glade air fresheners in the house that went off automatically, so it masked any unpleasant lingering evidence.

To add to my job list, around this time I also used to do a bit of window cleaning with a mate of mine.

My stepdad John, who saved me from getting exposed

It was an eventful experience cleaning windows with him. He was washing the windows on one house and it was a bit windy, so I was holding the ladders for him. He then stepped off the ladder and stood on the ledge on top of the door to reach another window. The ladders were sturdy as they were leaning on the wall beside the door, and he said to me "Daniel, can you go to the van and get me a couple of cloths?".

I said "No worries", so off I went. I brought the cloths back and he realised he needed another sponge. Again he sent me off:

"Daniel can you go to the van and get me another sponge?". I said "no worries", and off I went. As I get to the van, he shouts at the top of his voice *"Daniel!"*. I shouted back *"What?"*. He said *"Get them ladders back off them kids!!"*

The kids were running up the street with his ladders, so I started chasing them. They tried to swing the ladders towards me and hit me with them, so I moved back and only narrowly missed getting hit. As I lunged towards them and grabbed the ladders back, the kids panicked and ran off. I say kids, they were teenagers, with nothing else better to do. In a way I smiled to myself as I felt like I had just had a ladder match with them like they do on the wrestling.

So you get the picture, I have had my fair share of jobs over the years, and have now finally found one which I enjoy and am good at - comedy. I didn't want to go back to working these other jobs I have tried in the past if I didn't really have to. The truth of the matter is, I'm utterly useless at everything else, and if I'm not useless something happens which turns into a drama and disaster strikes. It's probably best for everyone's safety that I just stick to comedy. Fortunately for me at this point a couple of corporate Zoom gigs came in, so that ticked me over and things were starting to look up again. I couldn't have kept my positive mindset without the one big mantra that I stick to in life. There is one big belief that I strive to always keep at the front of my thoughts, and without it I think my life would be very different.

Episode 8 - The Positives

My Auntie Sylvie is 86 and lives in Fuengirola in Spain. She is the most positive person I know, and she once told me something once that I will remember and repeat it for as long as I live:

"Worrying is a waste of energy"

I think having a positive mental attitude has helped me massively during this pandemic and as my Auntie implied, worrying about things is never going to help a situation. I was a couple of months into lockdown and I was starting to get used to it. I had to remember that when challenges or obstacles arise, I needed to carry on fighting and to not worry or stress - it will only make things worse. My daily routine would consist of getting up, doing a workout, going for a walk, posting a video online (if anything topical and entertaining was happening that day), doing an online show and then going to bed. This was all keeping me going, but nothing beats working live and I was really missing it.

Whilst I was plodding along with my new daily routine that I had created for myself, I got a message on my Facebook page from a guy called Simon Lipson. Simon was on a show which we are all familiar with, 'Dead Ringers'. He was starting a podcast called "Making an impression", where he would get the best impressionists from around the UK and interview them about how they work and create content as an impressionist.

I was pretty flattered to be included in this, as the guests he had on were mega and ranged from Jon Culshaw to Rory Bremner and Alistair McGowan, to name a few. He even had top American impressionists on there including Jim Meskimen, Christina Bianco and Josh Robert Thompson. Many of these people who were guests are people who I watched on TV when I was a kid.

I had great fun doing that podcast and Simon is a lovely guy. We were discussing what techniques I use to create each character I do and how I develop each impression. I have never really had techniques; when I'm learning a new impression, I just tend to watch them on YouTube and it just comes. The best impressions I do are of my friends, or people who I spend a lot of time around, I end up picking their voices, catchphrases and mannerisms up. I listened to the whole series and I found it so interesting how other impressionists worked. One particular thing that stood out to me was when Schaeffer Bates was explaining how he starts off getting a voice, he looks right into the person's life, finds out where they were born so he can get the origin of their voice, where they are living now in case they have picked up some of that accent, and then gets into the character.

Although I have never met him, I think he is a great impressionist, and it's really worth checking out his stuff online.

Another story I heard was when Al Foran was talking about another impressionist, Conor Moore, who locked himself in a room until he got his Tiger Woods impression bang on. That is dedication.

After doing the podcast, I decided that as this was going to be the new normal for me for the time being. I started wondering whether I should I look into doing my own podcast: as many of you know, I do love to talk. I didn't want to do one about comedy though, so I thought it could be quite fun to do a pod about something else that I absolutely adore: MMA. I'm a big fan of MMA, but especially of the early days which I don't want to be forgotten. I thought I could call it 'MMA the Beginning'. The idea was to get all the legends from MMA who were in the first UFC and Pride events to talk about their careers and how not only MMA has changed but how the rules have changed.

I used to train in MMA all the time up until I started working away performing when I was about 17. Not only did I train but I also used to compete. I got a silver medal in the British championships for Ju Jitsu, which sounds really impressive, but there was only me and a couple of other guys in the tournament for my weight class, as back then no one was really doing Ju Jitsu and it wasn't as popular and publicised as it is now. I also competed in a few other forms of martial arts. I won a kickboxing competition in Sunderland, and a grappling submission fight where it was the best to 3 submissions. One of the submissions I won with was the 'neck crank', a move which is now banned because there are understandably more rules and regulations in place now to protect fighters from life-threatening moves.

I had built up to start competing in some MMA fights. My first one was in a Working Men's Club in Ferryhill, where I lost by split decision. I was 16 at the time and my opponent was 22. It was a 2x5-minute round fight and I was absolutely knackered by the end of it. In the break between rounds I was speaking with my coach John Dawson:

John: "How you feeling?"

Me: "I'm fucked"

John: "Are you going to give up then after all this training we have done?"

Me: "Am I fuck? Let's get this done"

This is why I have a hell of a lot of respect for MMA fighters, I think they are the best athletes in the world, and not only that but the toughest. I was absolutely knackered after the first round, but I managed to find my second wind for the second round.

My MMA days

The other fight I had was against a guy called Dave Metcalf, who basically outclassed me. He had me in side position and planted about seven elbows into my face before the referee stopped the fight. After this I realised that if you want to be an MMA fighter you have to want it so bad that you would do anything, and after that fight my confidence went. I realised fighting wasn't for me, because it's never really been in me. I love going to the gym and having a roll, but I don't have that fighting spirit in me. Many of the people who I trained with, who now compete, have it.

Also, deep down I've always wanted to be a comedian, as I have always had the pleasure of the feeling you get when you make people laugh. I am so pleased that I have had all those life experiences from fighting and training, because they have taught me determination, discipline and respect. It is now a hobby of mine, and I train for fun and fitness.

Anyone who doesn't know or doesn't want to know about MMA just assumes its 2 thugs in a cage or a ring wanting to rip each other's heads off, when in actual fact it is two very skilled and well-conditioned athletes, competing for something that they have both worked extremely hard for. If you work really hard for something it teaches you that life is not handed to you on a plate, if you don't succeed, you work even harder until you do succeed, and that is the attitude that I have taken into comedy.

So back to the podcast, the next step is figuring out how to get the guests?

Ken Shamrock follows me on Twitter, so I thought it would be awesome to get him on. In my opinion him and Royce Gracie are the pioneers of MMA, and made it what it is today. After a few beers and a couple of vodkas, I plucked up the courage to give him a message and ask him if he would come on. The next morning, I woke up and I told Aimee that I had messaged Ken Shamrock last night and asked if he would come on my first podcast.

Aimee: *"Why didn't you do it when you were sober?"*

Me: *"Well I thought it was the right thing to do at the time"*

Aimee: *"I bet the grammar was all over the place and it didn't even make sense"*

To be fair (as always) she was right, it wasn't the best worded message I have ever written, and there were a couple of spelling mistakes. That's one thing that I would say is a downfall of mine. I put things up on social media sometimes and don't check the details because I get the urge of excitement to post it. If I have a good idea, or if I think it's going to be a good video, I just post it without checking the grammar. More often than not it is all over the place, but I am always corrected - if not by Aimee, then by the 'grammar police' on Facebook. When I told Aimee I was going to write a book, we had a conversation.

Aimee: *"Well let me check the whole thing before you send it to the publisher".*

Me: *"they have people to check that surely?"*

Aimee: *"Well let's just be on the safe side, shall we?"*

When I write material, I just type away and wait to sort out all the grammar at the end. In fact, sometimes I don't even do that because if it's stuff I am writing for my stand-up routines there's only me who is going to read it anyway - and I know what I mean when I read it back.

I have always been a fan of Ken Shamrock ever since I first saw him on the WWE: he has always been a specimen of a man and in amazing shape. I was once watching the wrestling when I was about 13 with my cousin Ben and he told me that Ken Shamrock was a legit tough guy and fought in tournaments where people do this shit for real.

Back then we didn't have easy access to the internet, and it wasn't anything like what we have today. When we first got dial-up internet, it wasn't possible to make a phone call whilst using it - so internet time was limited, especially when my Mam was expecting a phone call. Imagine telling kids that now! Even 7-year olds have a mobile phone, it's crazy. After my cousin told me that, I wanted to find out about the fighting that Ken Shamrock was involved in. I was fascinated. I know now as an adult that wrestling matches have a pre-determined winner. By the way when I say a pre-determined winner, I don't mean in any way shape or form that wrestling is fake, it's well documented that pro wrestlers suffer with many injuries as a result of the bumps they have taken in the ring over the years.

So, from watching various documentaries I've seen how important it is to be careful with how you phrase things: the matches may be scripted, but the bumps, pain, risk and danger are real. One night I was watching Tonight with Trevor McDonald, and there was a section on the programme about extreme fighting. I saw a guy who was a monster, weighing about 600 pounds, getting dropped by a guy who was not even half his size. Me and my cousin Ben were sleeping at my Nana's house at the time. Although Ben is my cousin, we grew up spending a lot of time together like brothers would. Ben said to me "This is it…this is what I was on about, the fighting that Ken Shamrock does."

When I watched the documentary, there were people on there who wanted it banned. I didn't! I thought it was brilliant entertainment. I also think now that if anyone wants to put themselves in that position of danger in the cage then it's at their own discretion.

A few days later I was in town, in HMV, and something caught my eye. I saw a video in the pro wrestling section called 'Ultimate Fighting Championship - the challenger Ken Shamrock & the champion Royce Gracie'. My eyes lit up, this is what Trevor McDonald had given free advertising to. I wouldn't have known about it if it wasn't for his show. Nice one Trevor!

I was 13 and had no money, but I desperately wanted to buy it, and there was no way my Mam was going to buy it for me: it was an 18, and she was strict on stuff like that. It was 2 weeks before my birthday, so I thought if I wait I could get it with my birthday money. But then I thought what if someone buys it first? There was only that one copy on the shelf, so I went up to the guy and said:

Me: "Excuse me, I am not going to have any money until a couple of weeks' time and I want to buy this video, is there any chance you can reserve it for me? I definitely want to buy it"

Shop assistant: "First come first serve mate. Plus, it's an 18 and you're clearly not 18."

I was a bit devastated to be fair. I thought I am just going to have to wait for two weeks, and then I can try again when I get my birthday money. Once I had the cash, a couple of weeks later, I wasn't quite sure how I was going to get the video. My first thought was to ask someone if they could buy it for me and I'd give them the money. At the time there were kids my age asking people to go in a shop and buy them cider, so surely people wouldn't mind going in and getting me a video that's an 18 certificate.

Digressing a bit here but my auntie once told me that my Nana used to go in and buy people cider when they were teenagers as she didn't know cider was an alcoholic drink. Every Friday my Nana would take my auntie and all her friends' money, to go into the shop as requested, and buy them it, they told her they couldn't get it because they were all at netball practice, or something like that anyway, and they all like to have some cider on a Friday night. Every Friday my Nana would buy about 10 litres of cider and give it to my auntie and all of her friends. The people who worked in the shop must have thought my Nana was an alcoholic, and the funny thing about it is my Nana doesn't even drink alcohol: she has never touched a drink in her life.

So I had my birthday money and I was outside of HMV and I asked a couple of people if they could get me the video and they said no. My next plan of action was to look and see if the guy who told me I was too young to buy the video was working that day. He wasn't, so I went into the shop, got the video, took it to the counter and paid for it. Once I got out of the shop I felt like a dealer who had just smuggled a million pounds' worth of drugs through customs, I couldn't wait to get home and watch it. After watching it I became hooked, and became a huge fan of Ken Shamrock in particular. I then started going to judo classes, and then karate classes, and then eventually MMA. In hindsight, I was pretty obsessed.

The main reason I became a fan of Ken was because of what he had gone though in life, how he overcame it, and how he achieved his success. He is an incredible fighter who has great submissions, can wrestle and also strike: he was one of the first fighters who was an all-rounder, whereas a lot of fighters back then were just one-dimensional.

The morning after I had sent the message, me and Aimee were out on our daily walk when I got a notification on Twitter: "Len Shamrock has sent you a message". The message was simple: "Absolutely, let's do it". I couldn't believe it.

I called Kane from Joke Pit and explained to him that I wanted to do a podcast called 'MMA The Beginning' and I've got Ken Shamrock lined up as my first guest. I told Aimee that Ken had just messaged me and she told me to calm down and compose myself before I reply, and of course her famous words, "let me check the spelling and grammar before you send it." I said "Calm down? Calm Down? How would you feel if one of your heroes messaged you and told you they were happy to come on a podcast that you are going to do?"

She said "I get that, I am just saying let me check the message before you send it to him."

I sent Ken a message back asking him for his availability and he said he would be in touch. I was delighted. A couple of weeks passed and I didn't hear from him, I remember telling my mate's wife Kim about it and she said "Well message him again then, remember shy kids get no sweets." Kim is great, she's the wife of one of my best friends Anth. She's very honest and doesn't give a shit (I seem to know a lot of people like that). During the first lockdown we used to do a Zoom quiz (probably along with every other household in the UK) every Friday night. There would be Me and Aimee, Anth and Kim, Micky and Caroline, Andy and Laurie and Michael and Katie. It was nice because it gave us something to look forward to each week, but after the 100th quiz we were all quizzed out, something I'm sure you can all relate to.

So I took Kim's advice and I sent Ken another message. To be fair to Ken, he replied to me straight away and said "I have a lot on at the minute so just bear with me". That was understandable, because he is one of the biggest stars the WWE had, plus he's an MMA legend, so I can imagine why he would be busy and be in high demand. I was so grateful that he took his time out to do the podcast with me. He stuck to his word and we got it all organised. On the day we recorded the pod I was so nervous. I was sitting in the garden talking to Aimee beforehand, with all my notes prepared, and I had a drop of CBD oil to calm me down - and then a glass of wine to calm me down a bit more.

Kane logged us into Stream Yard and Ken's agent Jeremy was checking the sound at his end. We started recording and Ken came on the screen. I remember him getting into his chair like it was slow motion, as I still couldn't believe this was happening, this man who I was such a huge fan of since I was a kid was about to talk with me for an hour. It was a similar feeling to when I met Billy Connolly, I was pretty starstruck, but then as the pro in me does I got into it and the show opened with:

Me: "Mr Shamrock, how are you?"

Ken: "Good, how are you?"

Me: "Good, I believe you have been doing some filming for impact wrestling?"

Ken: "Yes"

A one-word answer. I realised that I needed to pick this up. I'd worked hard to get him on the show, and I needed to make this fun for both of us. I said:

"The reason I wanted to make this pod was because I was recently in Las Vegas and I was watching the Cerrone v McGregor press conference and I got talking to these guys who were sat next to me. They said the reason they got into MMA was because of Conor McGregor, I said to them have you ever seen the early UFCs like UFC one, and they said no. I was offended, Ken, I'm not going to lie."

He laughed, and right there I think he knew how much respect I had for him. He understood what we were going to talking about, and the ice was broken. The pod lasted for an hour and it was brilliant. Ken was just a great guy and eventually it felt like I was talking to someone I had known for a while. After the pod Kane said to me "Mate, that was incredible, like I can't explain how good that was."

It was scary at first but I think he warmed to me

Also that was my first time not only doing a podcast, but interviewing an MMA fighter. I was on such a high after, I remember doing the quiz that night and telling everyone about it. I was absolutely buzzing. I continued with a few more episodes of 'MMA The Beginning'. I had Vernon White on as another guest, who was actually trained by Ken Shamrock, and fought in the UFC. He was 'King of the Cage' middleweight champion, and just a lovely guy. He even carried on chatting to me for a bit once we stopped recording. I told him that I would love to go and do some training with Ken and asked him if it's advisable.

He said "You should be fine but if he tells you to put a headguard on just say no". We both laughed about it, but after we'd stopped laughing he said "No Danny, I'm serious, say no". I also got a friend of mine on – Bryan Lacey, who is a comedian. He is also a die-hard MMA fan, and is now a colour commentator who has worked alongside some legends like Frank Mir. Another guest I had on was John Dawson, who I mentioned earlier in the book and basically trained me since the age of 13. I have a lot of time for John, there were times when I had no money and he used to let me train for free if I had a competition coming up.

He is also such an interesting person: after training I would sit and talk to him for hours about martial arts. I also had Frank Trigg on the pod. Frank was a great guest and probably the easiest, as he just chatted away about his fights with Matt Hughes. Dana White, the UFC President, described it as the best fight in UFC history. Frank is now a stunt man in Hollywood, and an MMA official. We also still talk on social media occasionally. Stepping into the world of podcasts was something different for me and helped me to learn a new skillset. If it weren't for lockdown, I wouldn't have even thought about doing it. It was a positive experience and gave me a great sense of achievement. The podcasts are available on Joke Pit's YouTube channel and also on Anchor.

Another positive thing that came out of lockdown was when I got a text from a writer friend of mine, Christine Rose. She sent me a message saying that Jason Manford is doing a show called 'The Weekly Stand Up', and letting me know that she'd suggested getting me on the show. I thought great stuff. I met Christine via an agent called Lisa White who is a lovely lady and runs the 'Glorious Management' agency. Christine wrote a couple of gags for me when I was on BGT and she writes for all the top comedians on TV today. She was working on Jason's show. At the time there was also to be a fee involved, which was an extra bonus. She gave me Jason's email and I promptly dropped him a message. He replied asking me if I would like a spot on the show, which would be on August 6th. I obviously said yes!

I have always been a fan of Jason, because he just makes stand-up look so effortless. I am inspired by comedians who get you gripped by bringing you into their world, and Jason does that brilliantly. He did a very funny routine recently at the 2020 Royal Variety performance, where he was talking about the tier system that the government introduced. It was just so relevant and relatable, and had me and Aimee in hysterics.

In the weeks leading up to the show I would call friends of mine who are on the circuit as comics themselves to get their advice about what material I should do, as they have seen my set numerous times. I had a pretty good idea, but I just wanted to play it safe and get a second opinion. I spoke to Geoff Whiting, Miles Crawford and Paul Eastwood. They're all great comedians and great friends, and we go back a long way.

I also put my set past Christine, who hooked me up with the gig. She loved everything, but she did tell me to finish my set with an impression of Jason, rather than do it in the middle as I had planned. I already had a nice gag to finish on and the Jason material and impression I had wasn't as tried and tested, so I wasn't quite sure. She said to me "Danny trust me, finish on an impression of Jason, people will love it".

All of the people I have just listed have opinions that I value, so I felt a big sense of relief when they all more or less agreed with the material I had chosen. This Jason Manford gig was a big deal to me, and I didn't want to take any chances.

August 6th came along and I couldn't seem to log in to the Zoom link, and I started to panic. I thought this is just my luck: normally I get into Zoom meetings perfectly fine, and out of all the times for this to happen it happens when I have an opportunity that is going to further my career. I gave Debi a call, who had sent me all the information regarding the gig, and she was able to direct me to the right likes so that I got in fine in the end. I was as Aimee says "being a panachy poo". It was great because I could also watch other acts who were on the bill, so it was like I was doing a circuit gig from my own house.

It was time for my spot, and Jason introduced me: "I'm going to introduce to you now a comedian who we all love, because basically he impersonates all of our mates, Danny Posthill". I think that's the reason Geoff Whiting likes to book me, because when I do my set I impersonate most of the comedians that he has booked over the years who are now famous. The gig went brilliantly and I was delighted with it. When I finished on the impression of Jason it was just the icing on the cake. Afterwards I got a message from Christine which simply said, "Told you". I hate admitting that I am wrong, but on this particular occasion I didn't mind. I also spoke to Jason for a bit after the gig and he was very complimentary towards me. He was just an all-round lovely man, as I imagined he would be. I think being likeable on and off stage is a big part of being a successful stand up, and Jason is a prime example of that.

This whole experience was another great thing that came from lockdown. All of these things gave me more optimism for what was to come in the future, it felt like there were new doors opening for me, but who would be behind them and where would they lead me?

Episode 9 -
We're Back Open

It was the back end of June, and Boris Johnson had just announced that from July 4th the lockdown restrictions will be relaxed. Bars and restaurants would open, but with special measures put in place. No live entertainment was to be permitted, and 2-metre social distancing would be introduced as advised by the experts.

I didn't really know how to feel at this point. It was a bit frustrating as they were opening venues that I would normally perform in, but I couldn't perform. I was happy to be able to go to bars and restaurants again as it got us out of the house, and you could have a nice evening with friends and loved ones, bringing a bit of normality back into our lives. But when I was sat in these places, I was thinking to myself, how would a comedy night in this place increase the risk of Covid-19? Does laughter affect the immune system? Similarly, if performers sing will it really increase the risk of a socially-distanced audience catching Covid from one another?

There was talk that if you sing it can spread more germs because you are projecting your voice. In turn, tiny particles of fluid from the mouth had a higher chance of being spat out, projecting further and landing on someone. I understand that you have to look at the whole picture and take all factors that could increase risk into account, but as these people were all sitting at tables socially-distanced from each other anyway, I wondered whether it would really really make much difference if you just paid me some money, gave me a mic and I went and stood in the corner a few metres away for do my act.

How long would it be before we had our lives back, where we don't have to worry about social distancing, and we can continue entertaining people? Of course I was pleased that small businesses were getting back on their feet, but at the same time I was speaking to so many entertainers who were feeling down because they weren't working.

I would speak to quite a few acts around this time on a regular basis. I'd chat to Rudi West in particular maybe once a week, just to check in and make sure he was doing alright. I would actually ring round most of my comedy mates, as we were all in the same boat and understood each other's situation. The conversations all went more or less the same way: we would have a little rant about it all. Lockdown was easing, but we all felt ignored by the establishment, as if there was no way out for us.

Talking to Rudi always lifted my spirits. He is one of my favourite comedians; I remember watching him when I was 16 at 'The Engineers' Working Men's Club' in Hartlepool. He was a craftsman, and he was churning out laughs every 20 seconds with the whole room in stitches. You have to have an act that's bulletproof when you do the Working Men's Clubs, because people can be quick to judge and don't have a very good attention span.

Rudi would always say to me when I started out, "when you play clubs, they will stare at you with their arms folded thinking come on then, make me laugh". That's probably why Rudi's act was so polished, because he has played to so many bear pits. I've seen Rudi work a few times and some places I've thought to myself, how the hell is he going to turn this around? I would see some of the most hard-faced bastards you have ever seen, who you wouldn't even say excuse me to if you walked past them, because they looked like they would smash a glass over your head. But Rudi always manages to get them on side. Watching them laugh at Rudi's material just made me think "Wow, that's a comic right there" - it's like he hypnotised the audience with laughter.

The Working Men's Clubs may be hard places to play, but they are also places you can get some great stories from. My Uncle Paul has always drunk in them ever since I can remember, and he told me a story that happened to his mate one time at a club in Middlesbrough. Apparently, there was a water leak coming out of the toilets at the club, so they informed the doorman. The doorman said "Don't worry, I will get this sorted. I'll get Alan to deal with it, he's a plumber". The only problem was that Alan had been drinking all day, and had had about 10 pints by this point. This was the cheaper alternative to getting a plumber in to look at it, who was actually in working hours.

So Alan comes to investigate and is pretty hammered, but he assesses the leak and decides to go ahead and fix the problem. Everyone is stood around waiting for what the outcome is, and Alan comes out and tells everyone that he has fixed it.

Doorman: "Well what happened then?"

Alan: "What happened was someone pooed themselves because they didn't make it to the toilet in time. They've took their pants off and threw them down the toilet, then flushed the chain and that's why it started the leak, because the pants were causing a blockage".

Alan (again): "Oh, by the way, they were Calvin Kleins."

Doorman: "They were what?"

Alan repeated "They were Calvin Kleins"

Doorman: "Right, where's the members book? He's getting barred out!"

The doorman actually thought there was someone called Calvin Klein who was a member at the club. I wish I could have been there to witness this.

As restrictions were easing, after a couple of weeks, Aimee was going back to work, and at this time she was under contract with Butlins as part of the resident cast. She performed in various production shows with a cast of around ten performers. She had to go back earlier before the resort opened as they had to rehearse the shows, and re-block taking into account social distancing. Aimee went off to rehearse and I was left in the house on my own. In a way I quite liked it because I didn't have to worry about leaving my underpants on the bathroom floor, or my fork touching my plate to loudly whilst I was eating my dinner. But after a couple of days, I was missing her. I suppose that was the good thing about Covid, we'd got to spend more time together compared to normal, and when she left it made me realise that I was taking her for granted. We are usually like passing ships in the night, rarely in the house together as one of us is always on our travels, doing shows on the road.

When she went this time it made me realise how much I do love and miss her, sometimes you don't realise what you've got till it's gone. By being in lockdown together we also helped each other to have a more positive mindset, we did argue at times, but who doesn't when they're both locked up in a house together 24/7. I started to set myself more goals each day when she was away, otherwise I would just end up going to the pub all the time. I was exercising, and still doing some online work with Kane; the panel shows like "What gets my goat" were still happening, so that also kept my mind active, as I had to come up with things that were pissing me off each week.

To be fair, this was harder with Aimee being away. As much as I love her, I think it's easier to get pissed off when someone else is around you than if you're sat on your own. My focus was also gradually moving back onto live gigs, as there were now small allowances regarding live performances. You could perform outside, provided that social distancing measures were in place. Back at Butlins, Aimee's shows were being socially distanced and prepared to be performed in the Circus tent, which qualified as an outdoor space. At this time I had a few gigs booked in there for July and August, so that was some reassurance, as I could see there was progression from what was happening with Aimee's shows. I thought if they are using full-scale production shows, then surely my gigs should be on: at the end of the day its only me with a microphone talking, so it's probably the most Covid-friendly act you could find.

The first gig I done after coming back from lockdown was outside, and it was a great line up. I was on with Pat Monahan, who has been on the circuit for years, and is a seasoned pro. There was Steve N Allen from the Mash Report, and the headliner was Tim Vine who I love. His one-liners are so clever yet so silly. He's a really nice bloke too, and very generous with giving other comedians advice.

The only problem with the gig was it was a drive-in comedy, a first for me and probably most of the other comics, but this was the new norm. We had no choice, so people were sitting in their cars waiting for a show. My first thought was right, get through your material, time it as if you got a laugh, and move on to the next part of your act. It was surreal walking on to a load of cars beeping their horns at me, which actually gave me a nice opening line, I said "Thank you so much for that lovely introduction with you all tooting your horns at me, normally when people do that to me, I get road rage and tell them to fuck off!"

Keeping our distance

It turned out to be a really good gig, and there were people sat just outside of their cars as well, so at least you had some kind of verbal feedback. Tim Vine was on the bill after me, so when I did an impression of Tim followed by his brother Jeremy, it went down a treat.

I'm often asked how people react when you do an impression of them, because they probably don't realise that they do the things that you pick up on. Tim took the impression really well and after my set he said to me in a jokey way "Good impression, nice jokes too I should have wrote them down". Overall, it was just great to be back working with people in the flesh. One of my favourite things about gigging on the circuit with other comedians is you all have such a laugh backstage and it's quite often that when you're all having such a laugh in the green room together you feel like saying "I don't want to do the gig now, I'm having such a good time in here."

From then on things started to pick up. I did a local gig along the seafront at home, in Hartlepool, at a bar called Hornsey's. There was a dismal 16 people in, and unfortunately the weather wasn't great. It was a windy night and the people who were in had had a lot to drink, so I can't lie it was a challenge. I bantered for most of my set, and was getting my material in as and when I could. I was trying to remember my material but also to control 16 drunk people, and Aimee says I can't multitask! There were also people randomly walking in late who were pretty hammered, but fair play to Hornsey's though for trying to bring live entertainment back - they were one of the very few places who actually tried.

After that I had a phone call from an agent Marc Leyton, who deals with all my holiday centre bookings, and he offered me runs at Butlins Bognor and Minehead for September and October, plus a couple of extra gigs elsewhere. Marc is a great guy: what I like about him is that he is very up front and honest, that's why we have a good working relationship. Just as I felt things were looking up he did tell me that we could go back into lockdown again at any time, and there was a chance these gigs coming may be cancelled again, which was already at the back of my mind anyway. But on the positive side I thought for the moment, all going well. I had quite a few gigs in the diary, and I was going to be earning the money that I was previously earning. The gigs were to be inside and the audiences were to be socially distanced.

I was also told that I was not allowed to get the audience to cheer or interact, as when people shout it would spread more germs. Due to socially distanced audiences, it meant lower capacity in venues, which meant in order for all guests to see the show I had to do two spots instead of one. I wasn't complaining because I was thankful for the work and the money, but yet again this was a new norm we had to get used to.

Episode 10 -
Jim Davidson's Shows

During that time, I had a call from Jim Davidson who I have met a couple of times previously, mainly through me going to watch his shows because I am a fan - but I also did a gig with him entertaining the troops at Larkhill. The gig was outside and the soldiers were sat on haystacks while they were watching the show. Any comic will tell you that military gigs can be tough to do, but Jim handled it like it was a piece of piss, like he just popped on for a chat and ruthlessly annihilated them with his killer one-liners. The scary thing about it was I had to go on after him. I have a lot of respect for the Armed Forces, and I did that gig for free as it was raising money for charity.

He always makes me laugh

Soldiers don't just go through a lot when they are out on the battlefield, they often suffer terribly after with their mental health. Jim often raises money for PTSD and helps many of them recover from alcohol and drug issues. I can imagine when you see a fellow soldier getting shot on the battlefield you must go through a hell of a lot of trauma, which in turn is making them turn to drink and drugs through no fault of their own, simply to block the pain. I think we need to help these people a lot more and give them support and attention in return for the services they have provided for our country. It breaks my heart when I hear about ex-military living on the streets and suffering. What I've also found, mainly from being involved in these gigs, is that many soldiers have a dark sense of humour.

I discovered this after the gig with Jim, as I had another 'slave to my arse' moment. I needed the toilet (of course) and as it was an outside gig there were only porta loos. I was getting on with my business, but one of the soldiers must have clocked me going in because halfway through I felt it starting to rock, and straight away I realised those bastards are going to tip this over. Whilst I was mid-shit, I burst the door open and ran across the field like a penguin with my pants down to my ankles, the lads couldn't stop laughing. I pulled my pants up and ran to Aimee's car, which luckily wasn't far, and just by the backstage area. I made her drive me to the nearest toilets which were 2 miles away. I did see the funny side after, I mean it could have been worse, I could have tipped over, and God knows what would have landed on me, whilst wearing a new suit!

Jim called me up and asked me if I wanted to be a guest on his new chat show "Sunday Night Live", which is on his TV channel JDTV. This was the first time I had been to his studios, and I got to know him a bit better in comparison to the briefer encounters we have had in the past. He was really welcoming but I was also really nervous as Jim has seen a lot of comedians in his time so quite understandably, he will be hard to please.

Before the interview started he said to me "What shall we talk about then?" I said "We'll just wing it", he said "Ok", and before I knew it, he started to introduce me on. We were chatting away and he was feeding me impressions that he knew were in my repertoire and it flowed brilliantly. One voice in particular which went really well was of Nigel Farage, after the interview Jim's wife Michelle came up to me and said "Your Nigel Farage impression is amazing, we go out and have lunch with him sometimes and your voice and mannerisms were spot on". I take comments like that as a huge compliment because if you do an impression of someone they know personally it has to be spot on. I met Nigel a couple of times, and he knows I do an impression of him but I have never done it to his face. I wasn't sure whether he would like it, and besides, I didn't want to risk pissing someone off who just bought me a pint.

I'm sure he wouldn't take offence to it though as he's a man who has broader shoulders than most people. It is funny though when you look at how people take an impression. I remember when I used to impersonate my teachers when I was at school, word got around of who I could do and I'm sure they used to talk about it in the staffroom because one science teacher said he didn't want me in his class because he didn't want me to hear him speak. Unfortunately for him, he had no choice as he had to teach bottom set.

Jim more recently asked me onto his other new show, on his LMAO channel, "The Saturday Morning Picture Show", which is hosted by Miles Crawford, and features Bobby Davro and Vicky Wright. We filmed six episodes in 2 days and my sides were aching the whole time. It was a mixture of Gogglebox and a panel show where we watched cartoons and movies from back in the day and in between the movies and cartoons we would basically mess around and Jim would give us subjects to talk about. There was nothing really planned and we just milked it. I think it worked so well because we are all friends, you just feel more comfortable working with each other. I am not saying that I do not like working with people I don't know, but I just find it easier when you work with people you know, as there is less pressure and you relax more into it. I was also on his recent "Sunday Night Live" Christmas special, which was aired on Christmas eve, it is great to now have him as a contact and to be doing so much work for him.

On of my favourite things that I have seen Jim do is his adult pantos, there's a few people doing them now but no one does them like Jim, one scene in particular was when him and Charlie Drake improvised and Charlie Drake was pissed. Check out the clip it's on YouTube it was one of the funniest things I've ever seen. I've watched it so many times that I managed to learn Charlie's voice and there was one line he said in the panto which has stuck with me "Are you a fucking Pixie?"

In the scene Jim was trying to correct Charlie that the character he was meant to be saying his line to Mia Carla was playing wasn't a fairy, she was a Pixie and he basically blurted that line out randomly "Are you a fucking Pixie?". After me and my mate watched the Cinderella show, he got me to just randomly walk up to people in the playground at school and say to them "Are you a fucking Pixie?" in Charlie's voice and we would both crack up because some people didn't know what we were going on about, this was basically an in joke between me and him. One day he dared me to go and do it to my head of year and do it, which I did and as soon as I opened my mouth to do the impression, I immediately regretted it. He dragged me by my collar and sent me to his office. I thought "shit, this joke has gone too far" I was stood to attention in his office and he slammed his office door behind him. He then looked at me and said "Posthill do not ever do that to me again do you understand?" I said "Yes sir, sorry sir" He said "Do you know why you shouldn't do that again?" I said "Yes sir as it's very disrespectful" he said "Not only is it disrespectful it is also a brilliant impression, I saw the show and it was Hilarious and I was dying to laugh, but if I did it wouldn't set a very good example to the other kids, now go on scatter" I walked out of his office knowing that deep down I probably made his day. I done the impression of Charlie to Jim and he loved it as I think it took him by surprise. That's one thing that I didn't realise was so important about comedy: the element of surprise.

I remember Freddie 'parrot-face' Davies, a comedian who has been going for year,s once asked me when I met him "Do you know the most important thing about comedy? I said "Timing, Delivery?" He said "No, the element of surprise". Thinking about it, he's bang-on right because when you laugh at something it shocks your body because something happens that's so unpredictable it just hits that funny bone and taking Jim by surprise with the impression of Charlie did exactly that.

I have always loved Jim Davidson and the subjects he talks about; I just love how outrageous he can be. I once had to pause my DVD player because I was in fits of laughter at one of his routines, it was his routine about the first time a woman gives a blow job, and he used the microphone as a prop, my sides were killing me. The observations that he delves into when he's talking about certain subjects are just brilliant. The way he paints the picture and acts out the characters really draws you in, he is also brilliant at accents which adds to the whole story. Over the years to have been in theatres watching him, and to see how much he is loved by audiences, to watching his DVDs growing up, and keeling over with laughter, to actually being in his company, it was quite something. After being locked down for several months and now being back out and working with new people, seizing opportunities coming my way it felt like the only way was up, that was until it all came crashing down again.

Episode 11 - Get Back To Prison

I was relieved to have got through my run of gigs in September and October. I had a few bookings in for November, and a possible panto for December, which was constantly on and off the cards in line with the ever-changing rules and anticipation of there being more lockdowns to come.

In the end we were locked away again, put back in prison, back to square one. Once again the emails came back in thick and fast about the cancellation of gigs: 'Because of the new Covid regulations we are sorry to say the booking at X club is cancelled. bla bla bla'. After a while I got used to it, but that couple of months' worth of work did help me big time, both physically and mentally.

Back in lockdown meant back to queuing at the supermarket. I didn't experience much of that myself as Aimee does the food shop in our house. Thankfully panic buying wasn't happening as much this time round compared to the first lockdown. I did stock up on the toilet roll, but after reading through all these chapters about me being a 'slave to my arse' you can understand why.

I was sat there one day, back at home in what felt like my prison cell, reminiscing to myself, about all the gigs that I had done over the years. I also asked myself a question that I have never asked before:

"Why the fuck did I become a comedian? Or why would you even want to become a comedian?"

Is it the buzz from making people laugh? The attention? Making people happy? Or just because you want to be someone and you want to prove yourself in life, and do something that none of your mates are doing? I'm sure a couple of my mates from my childhood and growing up could have been comedians. I have spent days in the pub where my sides were aching with laughter, thinking why isn't this man a comedian?

Billy Connolly always said that he would laugh more at the guys he worked with at the shipyards in Glasgow than he would watching a comedian, which I completely relate to. So why do people go to comedy clubs? Why don't they just go to the pub with their mates and have a laugh every week? Debating all these questions, I think the reason people don't decide to take the jump and be a comedian is because it's such a risk. You have a lot to lose. You have to have so much drive, determination and confidence in yourself, and in my case right now I had to keep ploughing through because I had no choice.

I remember having this conversation with a guy in New York. To set the scene, me and Aimee had gone away to New York for a week. One day we were on the subway and got talking away, missed our stop, and ended up in Harlem. We needed to get off in Harlem to get back to the original stop we were supposed to get off at, which to be honest, I can't remember as Aimee was in charge of all this. When I am away on my own, travelling around the world doing gigs, I find my way to and from places no problem, but to be honest I do get sick of looking around and trying to figure which way to go: I'm very impatient. So when we are together, I don't really mind Aimee being a bossy boots. She has to take charge because she doesn't trust me, so with her oversized tourist paper map in hand, I just let her kick on.

I think it's also because I am so laid-back people can't get over the fact that I manage to get from A to B. If I need to do something, I just get on with it. I once broke my foot on a stag do in Magaluf. I then had to fly to Malaga to get to a gig, and did the gig with a broken foot. I didn't tell anyone because they would just worry. But when I tell people after they just look at me and say "You flew from Palma to Malaga and then did a gig with a broken foot? You went on with crutches?" I said "No, I got to the dressing room with my crutches, had 2 large brandys and an ibuprofen, walked on, stood in the same spot for the whole show and got through the pain". If I didn't do the show, I wouldn't have got paid, so in my eyes I had no choice. To be honest I didn't realise it was broken until I got home and had it X-rayed a week later.

As we found ourselves in Harlem, I wanted to take a look round.

Me: "I've never been to Harlem before let's get off"

Aimee: "No way Danny, it's meant to be really dangerous round here"

Me: "Come on let's have a walk around, it will be better as we will see more locals as opposed to tourists, and we will see how New Yorkers really live"

As we were walking through Harlem, I could sense that she was going to burst into a panic attack at any moment. I shouldn't have put her through it really, but at the end of the day she is with someone who has a rebellious mind, so she's only got herself to blame. It was quite scary to be honest, and I did feel like we could have got mugged at any moment, but I kept telling Aimee that everything was going to be ok. I told her to put her map away so we didn't look like tourists with loads of money in our bum bags. We ended up in this bar with a load of Italian guys sitting at a table having dinner and drinking wine. It felt like a scene from a gangster movie.

I thought 'this is great', but Aimee said to me "Come on Danny, I think we should go". I persuaded her to have just one drink, went to the bar and ordered myself a whisky and Aimee a gin and tonic. We sat on the high stools at the counter and got talking to the bartender, who was really nice. The guys overheard our conversation and you could see one of them in particular, the boss looking guy, looking over at us.

This guy shouted over to us in a thick American-Italian accent,

Him: "Hey! Where are you guys from, Ireland?

Me: "No across the border in England"

Him "Ok where in England?"

It felt like an interrogation rather than a conversation. By this point he had walked over and was stood between the two of us.

Me: "Hartlepool"

Him: "Where the fuck is that?"

Me: "It's a place in the North of England, a nice smallish town and they call us Monkey Hangers"

Him: "Monkey hangers? Why is that?"

At this point the whole table started to gather round us, and think Aimee was about to dial 911. But me being the good bullshitter that I am I answered his question with confidence, like I was doing a gig.

I told them how in the Napoleonic Wars, they thought there was a French spy trying to start an invasion. They couldn't understand a word he was saying, so they hung him. It turned out not to be a French spy, but actually a monkey. I told them about Hartlepool United's mascot, Hangus The Monkey – and how the person who used to be Hangus ended up becoming the Mayor because he promised free bananas if we voted for him. The moral of the story, I said, is never go on vacation to Hartlepool.

The guys all laughed and the boss guy introduced himself:

Him: "My name's Joe".

Me: "Great to meet you Joe, this is my fiancée Aimee"

Him: "Lovely to meet you both can I get you a drink?"

Me: "I'll have a whisky"

Him "You already got a full one there"

Me: "I know, but if someone kindly offers me a drink it would be extremely rude to decline"

Him: "I like that, what would your lovely lady want"

Aimee: "No its ok, I'm fine thank you"

Me: "Come on Aimee, he's offering us a drink, it saves us breaking into our holiday money. Get her a gin and tonic"

Him: "Coming up"

We had a laugh and they were great guys, they were also very loud, but I didn't mind that because it feels like I always have the best times in loud rowdy environments.

Me: "Would you guys like a drink?"

Him: "Why are you asking me if I want a drink?"

Me: "Because you bought me one"

Him: "Just because I buy you a drink doesn't mean you have to buy me one, are you stupid or something?"

**New York the day before
we met Joe**

I thought he was turning on me, there was a bit of a sour atmosphere and everyone went quiet. At this point I could tell that Aimee just wanted to be on a flight home. I said that I was just being polite, that's all.

He looked at me, they all looked at each other, and they all started to laugh, and then so did I, with relief. I'm surprised Aimee wasn't going to the chemist and asking for some beta blockers. I bought them all a drink and everyone relaxed.

Him: "Hey Danny I bet I can tell what you do for a living just by what you're wearing"

Me: "Go on then"

Him: "You work in finance"

Right there I knew he was full of shit because I was wearing a tracksuit.

I eventually told him what I do, and he did say to me that he wasn't surprised because he thought I was funny, which I thought was nice. After that Joe didn't let us buy any more drinks and it was probably one of the best days I had. It was time for Joe and the boys to go.

Him: "Danny, I got to go now, but can I just say that I've had a great day and you are a really lovely couple, but can I just leave you both with a bit of advice?"

Me: "Yeah go on"

Him: "A good relationship isn't perfect, it's gonna be good and it's gonna be bad, probably 80 percent good and 20 percent bad. No relationship is 100 percent perfect, and if anyone tells you that they are talking complete bullshit. A good relationship is 80 percent good and 20 percent bad. My relationship is the other way around, that's why I'm in this bar 80 percent of the time."

The place erupted with laughter, as though he was a comic finishing on his last routine and getting a big laugh to end his act. He left me with this:

Him: Keep doing what you're doing Danny! Do you know why you're doing what you're doing, and you keep working hard?

Me: "Tell me"

Him: "Because you have no choice"

I will always remember that, and that is the point that I am making. When it comes to doing comedy, once you commit and you have led yourself down that road for so long, you have no choice. You just have to carry on working hard because you don't have anything else to fall back on.

I would love to see what Joe is up to now and how him and his family are getting though this pandemic. We didn't exchange details which is a shame, but Joe If you manage to read this book please get in touch with me via social media.

This was when I was thinking to myself maybe I should have had a backup plan. All my mates who are electricians and plumbers were all working throughout the pandemic, and I felt like I should have trained myself in one of these trades in my younger days. You should always be prepared. But then again if I'm honest how can you prepare yourself for something like this? You would have had to put all the money you earn into savings. Fuck that, I like my holidays. I like going out and enjoying myself. Money comes and goes but memories don't.

If I had put all my money away and didn't spend anything, I wouldn't have had these experiences, like meeting Joe, which was really random - but pure gold. Sometimes I think you can go through life being too safe, but life is for living. You can have all the money in the world, but when you're locked down in your house you can't spend it on anything except food and bills. The memories I've had from doing comedy have given me some great laughs, especially the shit gigs. At the time it was soul-destroying, but now looking back it was funny.

When I was starting out a lifelong mate of mine Simon Hanlon used to drive me to some of my gigs, as at this point I couldn't drive. It took me a while to pass my test, and this is no joke. I had two hundred driving lessons because I was deaf in my left ear and my driving instructor was deaf in his right ear. If I drove in any other country, I would have been fine. Funnily enough, the first time Aimee told me she loved me was when we were in a horse and cart in Great Yarmouth and I just didn't respond. She felt pretty down, until she realised that she'd said it in my deaf ear.

So, Simon took me to this one gig at Thorpe holiday park. I was 19, it was a packed room, and I basically died on my arse. At the end of my set, I said "Ladies and gentlemen thanks for ignoring me, *you've been an audience,* Simon start the car"

I was backstage waiting for his car to pull round so we could make a quick getaway and he was taking ages. Ten minutes went by and he's still not there, so I thought I'd give him a call.

Me: "Mate where you at?"

Him: "I'm in the venue"

Me: "I told you to start the car so we could go"

Him: "Ah sorry mate I thought you said start the clap"

As if he was sat there clapping on his own when everyone else wasn't, now that is a mate. We still laugh about that story to this day.

My cousin Ben used to drive me to some gigs too. One time I did a gig and I thought it went quite well, until the end when we tried to take the speakers out to load the car up and they locked us in.

Me: "What's going on?" Me and my cousin thought we would have to fight the whole pub.

Landlord: "You have to apologise to Steve over there who you have taken the piss out of all night, otherwise you're not leaving"

Me: "But he was heckling me all night, what was I meant to do?"

The whole place went silent and stared at us. I have a bit of MMA training and our Ben used to box, but there was no way we were going to deal with 40 people in a backyard boozer, plus I hadn't been paid yet and I needed the money. I went up to the guy and apologised to him. The guys paid me, opened the door and let us out.

I started out doing comedy and singing, but I didn't really find myself as a comedian until I started doing the comedy circuit, so in a way I didn't really make the right decisions at the start of my career. At the same time it toughened me up, so when I went onto the comedy circuit in 2013 I had a wealth of experience behind me. Being locked down again made me think of all the shit I have put myself through, and now I can't even work. Was it all just a waste of time?

Episode 12 -
Mental Health

Wherever there is uncertainty, anxiety follows. Too much anxiety can lead to mental health problems. There's not enough said on the mainstream media about the stats on mental health. Day after day, we'd see the figures for Covid cases, but the mental health cases don't seem to be as well documented. It is a complex topic and there's a difference between mental health and mental illness, but it's important to do what we can to maintain a healthy mind.

From my experiences, and those of other people I know well, it's easy to turn to alcohol, food or drugs to try to forget about the external factors that are out of our control. At the time of writing, we have very little control. That's why so many are suffering from indirect effects of Covid-19: not working, not being able to see loved ones, young children stuck at home with parents not seeing their friends. It can put a strain on parents having to home-school and on children who are frustrated, not understanding why they've had to suddenly go from socialising to lockdown. I wonder whether there will be long-term effects of the missed education on future employment prospects.

In the first lockdown, I was drinking too much, more than I normally do. At first, I did limit myself to only drinking on the weekend, then it became Thursday-Friday-Saturday-Sunday, and then I added Wednesday. I realised that I needed to get a hold of this, because it could easily get out of hand and I'd end up drinking every night.

When that stopped, instead I was eating more takeaways and junk food to fill the void. All these things are something to look forward to, because let's face it, nice food makes you happy. When have you ever been sitting with your other half, and been watching a film and you say, "Oh I've just remembered we got some kiwi fruit in the fridge" and you run to the kitchen in excitement over the thought of indulging in such a healthy fruit, full of vitamin C? As much as I like kiwi fruit, I only eat it because it's good for me. Offer me a bar of chocolate instead, and I'm going to take it, because it tastes nice. What makes you happy makes you fat, but then when you become fat you end up depressed. It's a vicious cycle.

People can use alcohol to take the edge off life, because they struggle to face reality, and it's an escape route to try and forget about your problems. On the flip side, every time I go out and drink alcohol, I have a great time. I'm not always in the best mood the next day on a hangover. Alcohol is a drug: you go up, then you go down. People have used alcohol in this pandemic because we look forward to that feel-good moment it gives us for a short period of time, and it helps us to forget our problems. If we overindulge and have a little too much to drink, we expect the down state the next morning. The negative spiral continues: our body craves junk food, so we eat some whilst watching a series. That leaves you unable to be bothered to do anything, which leads to feelings of guilt about doing nothing constructive with your time, and then you start beating yourself up about it.

When you're beating yourself up, you'll go 'fuck this' and head to the shop for a bottle of wine (well I do anyway), it helps to wash away the guilt and you're right back at the start of the cycle again. This only happened to me for a few days, but I made a point of doing something about it, and I'm glad people like Kane from Joke Pit are around to give me a kick up the arse and stop me from being lazy, otherwise I could have quite easily fallen down this slippery slope. It also helps that Aimee isn't a big drinker, so she often keeps me on the straight and narrow.

I'm not saying I am cutting out alcohol completely; like most people, I enjoy a drink. I have started to do a once a week treat day where I allow myself a takeaway and a few glasses of wine because it gives me something to look forward to. You also enjoy it more because you're not having it as much.

There are certain alcoholic drinks that I am surprised I still occasionally drink. I'm sure we all have those drinks that we can't go back to after a traumatic session on it. For me, they're Baileys and tequila. When I got my GCSE results my mate Jamie was celebrating, and I was just helping him celebrate, because I didn't really get the best results. I was happy to just go along with it. We had a bottle of Baileys and I was throwing my guts up, mainly because I didn't drink at all then, so it clearly didn't agree with me. I have always been cautious of it ever since. I wouldn't turn down free booze, so if someone around me is having one then I might join them, but I tend to still get that sickly feeling when I drink it.

Then there's tequila. Holy shit, that was a drink that made me really ill. A lot of people don't know this story, and my family are probably reading this thinking oh for fuck's sake here we go, but I want to share. I was doing an adult panto called "Alad in Trouble", which was an adult version of the story of Aladdin. It was for a company called 'Fame Factory Spotlight'.

Scott Clarkson was the owner of the company, and at the time we were great friends. Scott and I first met a couple of years before when we were doing pantomimes round Working Men's Clubs when I was 18, for a guy called Gerry Graham. That was hard work: we would be doing three shows a day, all in different venues. We'd have to get there, put up the speakers and the set, do a 2-hour show, get all the stuff down, put it back in the van, get to the next venue and do it all over again.

Scott once told me a story from a previous tour he had done where they were on their way to the third gig of the day and the driver needed to go to the toilet, but they didn't have time as they needed to get to the show. Scott told him to piss into a bottle. As the guy was driving, Scott and the rest of the cast turned away so the driver could do his business into the bottle. As the driver was pissing into the bottle he had that sense of relief, as you do when you have been busting for the toilet and you finally go. Just as he felt that moment, he failed to notice the speed bump ahead of him. When he unexpectedly hit that, his willy flew out and he pissed all over the van. The whole unimpressed cast were covered in piss and they had another show to do.

We finished rehearsals for the adult panto and our first show was to be in Filey. Our 'digs' were at the parents of one of the cast members, Rob. His mum Pauline was lovely and looked after us with sandwiches and drinks. His dad Phil was basically there to help us along with the partying. Scott bought two bottles of tequila and he had decided that me and him were going to have a drinking competition. He had his bottle and I had mine, and we were to do a shot at a time, last man standing style. We were going shot for shot and then eventually we were both halfway down a bottle of tequila and I started to heave, so I went to the toilet to throw up and Scott was declared victorious.

I went to go to bed and I was so drunk that I went to climb on the top bunk and the bunk beds fell on top of me. luckily the wall was there to stop it from falling all the way and potentially doing real damage. Apparently, the rest of the cast including Scott were trying to get into the room but they couldn't. I couldn't remember any of that later.

Rob said to Scott "Shit, what if he's dead?". I did laugh when Rob told me this, because he does have a dark sense of humour, but what made me laugh even more was when I heard that Scott replied "Shit…..if he is we'll have to try and get another Aladdin for tomorrow".

They managed to get into the room and they got the bunk beds back upright and I was there on the floor and thankfully wasn't dead. I woke up feeling like I had died and just about come back to life. I honestly didn't think I was going to be able to do the show, but as soon as I walked on Dr Showbiz kicked in and I just got on with it. At one point I did miss half of the script out, but what do you expect when you get that drunk the night before?

I found out later that Scott filled his bottle up with water whilst I was drinking tequila, very naughty! To be fair I should have been more switched on to ask him why we were drinking out of separate bottles, so it was partly my fault for being so stupid. It does make you wonder why I still drink after stories like that. The number of times I see on Facebook people saying things like "never drinking again", but the next week we still do.

One thing I did make sure to do when I was at my height and drinking four nights a week was exercise. Even with a hangover, I would still do a Joe Wicks workout, or go out and do 16 to

20k on my bike. I was doing it, but I wasn't enjoying it, which obviously makes it a lot harder. I was doing it because I felt like I had to do it, just to balance out my lifestyle, plus I thought it was helping with my mental health. In actual fact it probably wasn't when it was combined with all the bad I was putting into my body. I was also putting weight on, even though I was exercising, proving the old saying "You can't out-train a diet". So along with making healthier food choices, I feel like walking is great for your mental health. With my D in GCSE Science, I don't have any scientific explanation, but I do know that after a walk I always feel great. I'll listen to some music or a good podcast as I'm walking, or make some phone calls and have a nice catch-up whilst I'm getting my steps in. Because I'm wearing earphones and have my phone in my pocket, I get the occasional "Sorry mate, what did you say to me?" as I walk past people.

It's funny. because now we all have a lot more time on our hands it can be difficult to get off the call. Normally I would say "I've got to go because I'm just at the Post Office" or "I've got to go as I'm just about to head to a meeting", but what can I say now? My mate Dave doesn't mess around. He never has, he'll just say "I'm going now Danny because you're boring me". I'm sure we all have mates like that – I know the things I've written about him might make him sound like he's my personal bully, but that's just the way we talk. He's a great friend.

Another friend of mine Christian Grant comes out with stuff on Facebook that people would be shocked by. The comments he makes he sounds like an absolute dick, when in actual fact he's not, he just likes to take the piss. I once put a picture up when I was at a high-end gig in London, and Christian just commented "No one cares where your gig is, stop craving attention". He then ended up getting himself into a confrontation with a few of my other friends along with my Mam. I had to explain to them that he was joking and that's just how he is.

As well as walking going out on my bike is also a nice release, we actually have some decent routes to ride round near our house. In particular going along the seafront and to the Marina is nice, though it's obviously better in the summer when the sun is shining and you can stop off for a drink. I was out on the bike over Christmas and I couldn't find my gloves, so I just grabbed Aimee's mittens from the cupboard. I was riding past a couple of teenagers and one of them shouted, because I had my helmet on (and rightly so).

"Can you not ride your bike properly mate?"

I was going too fast to have a comeback for them, and I couldn't be bothered anyway, so I just stuck two fingers up at them. Soon after I realised that it wasn't an insult to them at all because I had a pair of bloody mittens on. This is what happens when you're in the zone and you're preoccupied.

So far this year I have cut back on the drink and I have been eating healthier. I feel much better for it. Like I did at the start of the first lockdown, I make sure I have structure to my day, and I have things to do. My mind is constantly active and that's what I think is the game changer. It is natural that over the last year or so since everything we know has changed, our minds wander, our motivation changes, and we are all going to be riding the corona rollercoaster, and riding it at different times and speeds. We are not going to feel positive and motivated every day, just like the down not so good days aren't going to last forever.

By the way, I am just going from my own experiences regarding mental health, some people of course may have a different outlook, but I can only speak on my behalf. I just want to make that clear, so that the critics out there don't start telling me to stop lecturing people on mental health! I'm just explaining my slant on it, and discussing the techniques I use to help me keep a healthy mind. Mental health has more recently made its way into the media, and I think it's great that we now have an ongoing dialog, reassuring people that it's good to talk. For some people it is a struggle, and for others it is bubbling away and under control, but for the majority I believe it's trying to see the good in everyday and creating our own techniques and habits to assess how we are feeling, and what we can do to improve our daily mood and mental state. As a performer I think that I am so used to being in front of an audience, and surrounded by people, that it just doesn't sit right to be doing nothing, living a monotonous life, socially distanced from everyone. The key for now is to keep plodding through, and remain hopeful that life will go back to complete normality as soon as possible, but on top of that there is also the worry of catching Covid-19. As we know people's symptoms really vary, how will any of us know how our bodies will react until it happens, I've always been quiet accident prone, when I tell a story people are never surprised as of course if it would happen to anyone it would happen to me, which is actually quiet scary.

Again in the words of Auntie Sylvie "worrying is a waste of energy", but this really could be life or death, little did we know that a positive Covid test result was just around the corner.

Episode 13 - Aimee gets Covid

After the announcement around the end of October, telling us that we would soon be going into another lockdown, my gigs were all cancelled again. Aimee was also on her way back home from working in Skegness, and her shows could no longer go ahead either. When she got home we had a takeaway and watched a film, as usual when we haven't seen each other in a while. We were sat on the sofa watching a film when Aimee got a text from her group chat saying that another two people in her team had tested positive for Covid. The NHS track and trace message telling Aimee to self-isolate soon followed. The first question I asked Aimee was if she was feeling ok.

She said she was fine, but then I didn't want to make too much of a big deal of it and start to worry her or put anything into her head. The mind is a powerful thing and you can sometimes think there is a symptom there when you are maybe just manifesting it. I thought if Aimee does have it, we have been in close proximity since she has been home, so then I will probably get it too.

We woke up the next morning and we were both looking at our phones. We hadn't seen each other for a month, but it was still the first thing we did when we woke up. This is the world we are living in right now, and I am so guilty of it. My face is in my phone all the time. Aimee is constantly telling me off for it: I will check my email and texts, then my Facebook, then Twitter and finally my Instagram. If I do a video which starts to get loads of likes and shares, I'll be checking my phone every ten minutes. No wonder people suffer from mental health problems, because they are just watching other people's lives on social media and comparing it to their own.

Aimee was checking her WhatsApp group and learned that a few more people in her team were coming down with symptoms and going to get tested. I asked her again how she was feeling, and she again told me that she felt fine.

We carried on our day as normal and Aimee made breakfast. As she was excited to be home and back in her own kitchen, she went all out and made one of our favourites: eggs benedict. I was getting tucked into my food and Aimee asked me if it was nice, and of course I said yes. She took another mouthful of food and said "It's not as nice as normal, it's so bland. Don't you think it's bland? I feel like I need more salt and pepper on it."

We didn't think anything of it and carried on eating our breakfast. She then put even more salt and pepper on to try and make it taste better, but I thought it was fine. She asked me again if mine tasted nice. I said "yeah its lovely". To be honest though, with me I put loads of tomato sauce on my food, so that's probably all I can taste. I just think when it mixes in with the eggs it tastes lovely. I do love my condiments.

Suddenly it clicked. She said "Oh my God I'm so stupid, this is one of the symptoms of Covid, you lose your taste." She knew straight away she had it. Everyone from her work was getting it, and as much as they were following social distancing, this is the nature of the virus. It's highly contagious. They were working together, performing shows and sharing changing rooms (all socially distanced), but there is only so much you can do. They were sometimes in work from 10 in the morning until 11 at night, respacing and performing up to five shows a day. They were working bloody hard in order to allow all guests to see the shows and to give them a good experience. It was only a matter of time: once one person in the team caught it, it would be hard to break the circuit, especially as they were sharing accommodation as well.

Aimee booked online to get a test straight away, and as I was in the same household there was an option for me to get one too. As we had been in close contact I thought it was best to be safe. It was such an efficient booking process, and within the hour we were in the drive-through test centre taking our tests. We were in and out, and the next day the results came through. As expected, Aimee tested positive, but to my surprise I tested negative. I was confused by this but relieved at the same time, my worry now though was Aimee and I was hoping that her symptoms wouldn't get worse.

As Aimee tested positive, we both had to self-isolate for the next two weeks. We had enough food to last us and we both agreed that we were to eat healthy and make sure we were taking as many vitamins as possible to boost our immune systems. We also kept off meat and dairy as we got brainwashed from watching "What the Health" and "Game Changers" on Netflix: when I watched those programmes, I thought to myself how am I still alive?

Days One and Two for Aimee mainly consisted of headaches, loss of smell and loss of taste. She found the loss of taste was the most frustrating as during these two weeks the only real enjoyment she had was food, but she couldn't even taste it, so what was the point?

Like me she loves her food, so she was also worried as there were stories in the media of people who didn't get their taste back. Every day she would do a taste test of some kind. On around Day 3, Aimee woke up in the middle of the night in agony. She had terrible back pain, mainly in her lower back. It was around 3 am and she couldn't get comfortable, so she got up and sat in the chair for a while, then took some painkillers and managed to get back to sleep. The back pain lasted on and off for about two days, easing a bit after lots of hot water bottles, paracetamol, and ibuprofen. Since then, most of the people Aimee has spoken to who had Covid-19 suffered with body aches and pains of some kind.

As much as we were trying to be healthy, Aimee was trying everything in her power to get her taste back. Her preferred taste test was eating chocolate (what is it with women and chocolate?), and there was still nothing. I've mentioned before that Aimee isn't much of a drinker, and when she does drink it tends to be gin or vodka.

She can't stand wine. Whether it's red wine, white wine, rosé, champagne or prosecco, the taste and smell of all of them make her gag. She can't even handle it watered down with lemonade. I gave her a bigger taste test: could she take a swig of the half-bottle of wine left in the fridge? She swallowed a mouthful in a desperate attempt to get her taste back, but still there was nothing. In some instances, the loss of taste worked in my favour. Not in the way you're thinking you dirty bastards, but because I am a shit cook, and for this week it really didn't matter what I put on her plate.

Eventually, Aimee's taste and smell returned, so she unfortunately she now had to taste my horrendous cooking, which is something that I still haven't managed to master. The aches and pains disappeared, and she slowly got her energy back, taking it day by day. When she did get back to doing some online fitness classes, she was exhausted and breathless very quickly, which I think we both underestimated. It just shows how complex, yet incredible the human body is. I am pleased to let you all know that she fully recovered and got back to full health. Getting through Covid-19 now meant one less thing to worry about, and it was a strange feeling that Aimee was now one of those Covid case statistics. When we all look back in years to come this will be a moment in history, one of the biggest hardships that we had to face as a society in our lifetime.

It's a story to tell generations to come. The thought-provoking thing is that at the time of writing we don't yet know how the story ends, but there has to be a light at the end of the tunnel, doesn't there?

Episode 14 -
Light at the end of the tunnel

I'm writing this during the third lockdown. Going forward with this pandemic, I am starting to feel more optimistic. I feel that when we were in the first lockdown there was so much uncertainty and it was harder to stay positive, whereas now I think there is a light at the end of the tunnel. The vaccine is out and in circulation now, which certainly gives more hope for a brighter future. Many have suffered terribly in various ways over the past year since Covid-19 has entered our lives, and all I can do is express my deepest sympathies and send all my love to those affected, as well as my appreciation and thanks to all those working in the NHS and on the front line. Moving forward the only option we have is to keep a positive mindset, and count our blessings.

For me personally, despite having my whole career put on hold, during what felt like a momentous time, I have managed to branch out and do things I was unable to do when I was constantly on the road. It's actually nice to get up on a morning and look through the news and write topical material, not only that, but learn new voices. You can't really do that when you are in a packed train carriage travelling from gig to gig: you would get some funny looks. I have also had mates messaging me with ideas for videos that they want me to do, so I had time to make these videos at my leisure.

Recently a friend of mine, Matt Bourne, sent me a message saying Joe Wicks must be pissed right off now with another lockdown coming up, and that gave me a great idea to do a sketch. I did Joe Wicks in my set before lockdown but he didn't seem to be as well-known back then, but with him doing workouts for the nation and being a household name, it is the right time to put videos of him out. It's always great to get a character in the bag who everyone knows. Because there are so many channels, it's much more difficult these days to find people who everyone knows. With so many random people becoming famous via social media, it's tough to keep track. When you do voices you try and find those characters that no one else is doing, but they also need to be really recognisable. Joe Wicks ticks all of those boxes. Alistair McGowan once said to me that when you do a new voice, it's like hitting a tennis ball as the ball is coming up. You have to hit it at the right time to get the full effect.

I have tried to get people out there like Jordan Peterson and Ben Shapiro, who have great voices and characteristics. They basically have the whole package for any impressionist to impersonate them, but they are not as well recognised by the wider audience. Don't get me wrong, those people are massively famous but only within a niche market. I can imagine people are reading this thinking, "To be honest Dan, I don't know who either of those people are", but when people do recognise them, they absolutely love the impression.

If I do Conor McGregor in a comedy club, maybe twenty percent of the audience will know who he is, but if I do him at a sportsmen's dinner, I rip the roof off the place. As famous as Conor is, he is also very niche. One of my favourite characters I was doing during lockdown was Joe Exotic from Tiger King. At one stage he was massive, but within months he became old news, so I had to drop him from my repertoire. It's a bit frustrating when this happens, but it's all part and parcel of being an impressionist.

I always find it interesting chatting with other impressionists. I was fortunate enough a few years back to have a good chat with Mike Yarwood, and we compared the art of doing an impression now, compared to when he was on TV. For the people who don't know who Mike Yarwood is, he is probably the first person to bring fame to the art of impressionism. He had his own show every Saturday night for many years, and to me he is the godfather of impressionists.

I met Mike via Bobby Davro, once again Bobby saved the day and got me to meet yet another one of my heroes. Mike loves Indian food and Bobby was to meet him along with Jon Culshaw, who I also have massive respect for. I think Jon is a great technician and what I love about Jon is his approach and how he manages to find that 'hook', which is really difficult to find when you first learn a voice. A hook is a phrase or word you use to get into a voice.

People don't realise how long it takes to get a voice right, but I'm not going to lie, I do get quite lazy at times. I will start off with good intentions and watch people until my eyes bleed, but if I can't get the voice, I will leave it and maybe go back to it another day, instead of torturing myself and persisting with it. I would rather not dwell and worry over it, so in the end it can sometimes take a matter of days or even weeks until I am happy with the voice. What I like about Jon is that he has a quick turnaround. He gets the voice within a couple of days sometimes, and he always seems to manage to pull it off, which I find quite incredible.

Four generations of impressionists

So there I was with Jon Culshaw, Bobby Davro and Mike Yarwood: four generations of impressionists in an Indian restaurant (it sounds like the start of a joke). It was so surreal - how often would this happen in my life? It was crazy! I found Mike really approachable. To me it was like meeting Royalty and he came across to be the god that me Bobby and Jon looked up to. It was like we were at a service for impressionists. I just loved the fact that we all had so much respect for him and what he had done, but especially how he put impressionists on the map. As much as he was such a lovely guy and everything that you would want one of your heroes to be, I also had that apprehension in me that I was afraid he wouldn't approve of an impression if I did one in front of him. I did end up doing a few impressions as they came up in the context of the conversation, and my Trump impression made him genuinely laugh – which was a huge relief as it was like getting approval from the top of the tree.

There was a question I have always wanted to ask Mike and I managed to get it in.

Me: "Mike, there's a question I would love to ask you, do you think it is easier now for impressionists, as we have easy access to footage to learn new voices, or do you think it was easier to do it back when you were on TV and there were only channels 1 2 and 3?"

Mike (immediately, without any hesitation): "Easier back then when I was doing it because everyone knew who I was doing".

Joe Wicks, Ben Shapiro and Conor McGregor all have that one thing in common: there is such a wide pool of people to choose from to impersonate, that you have to make totally sure you pick the right person for your audience.

Being locked up has provided me with opportunities that otherwise wouldn't have existed; I would have never created a podcast, and to top it off I wouldn't have even dreamed of having Ken Shamrock on as a guest. He would have been far too busy if it wasn't for lockdown. The weekly Stand Up show with Jason Manford wouldn't have even existed, and comedians have a lot to thank Jason for, for giving us that opportunity, as there were so many comics out of work. As much as it was only one gig they got offered, it was one gig that they would have never got. With that Jason is now aware of who I am, and with someone like him letting me on his show and giving me that little bit of exposure has helped me massively for when we get back out there again. Who knows what else is going to come along?

I only met Jim Davidson a few times pre-Covid, but after I went on his chat show the first time he has had me on another chat show since, plus a series on his TV channel called "The Saturday Morning picture show", and who knows what the future holds with that?

It's always great when you get on with your heroes. Looking back from having to sleep in a sauna to now, the variety of people I have met is quite incredible. I'm not just talking about my heroes, but every person I have met who has helped me in some shape or form along the way. If not for Covid I also wouldn't have met Kane from Joke Pit and got more of an insight into building an online audience. My Facebook page is now monetised so I can earn money from my videos. In turn, everyone you meet can lead you onto meeting someone else. Whether it's in a professional or personal context, this is how we continue to grow as people, and in my case as a performer.

As much as we all need money to survive, lockdown has reminded us that money can't always buy you happiness, and as long as we are healthy that is most important. Most of the work I have done online over the past year has not earned me any money, but I feel that people who were not aware of me before now know who I am. I have even had other comedians ask me why I put videos online for free, telling me that it's just a waste of my talent.

Personally, I don't think it is a waste. It has definitely opened more doors, and most importantly kept my mind active and stopped me from dwelling on all the negativity around us. My job during lockdown, as we all know, isn't essential. Comedians and entertainers may be 'non-essential workers', but what is life without this art form? We need entertainment to give us an escape, to bring us joy and happiness, to make us feel and to emote us, and the most relevant to me, to make us laugh.

My conclusion to all this madness is that a negative attitude is no good to anyone. Stay positive, work hard and things will come good for you in the end. I have also written a new show which I can't wait to get out there as soon as venues open. I love trying out new stuff, it's nerve-wracking and exciting at the same time. I quite often do this at a local venue 'The Pot House' in Hartlepool, where I try out four different new 15-minute routines. It's great that I can try new stuff out locally and don't have to travel hours to potentially die on my arse. I also record it so I can go away and see what material hits and what doesn't, and that's when I start to make my cuts. After I have done that with all my 15-minute routines I will piece it together and take it to venues where I preview my hour.

I will then repeat the process and record that, make more edits, and add a few more bits in until I am happy with it. When you do impressions, you have to remember that people can go out of date very quickly these days, so you have to be prepared to just drop people even if you think the routine is landing. Once I am happy with the new show I have created, I am planning to take it to Edinburgh. To all my fellow entertainers out there,

I understand what you are going through and I feel your pain, but we will all get through this and be back doing what we do best very soon.

You may even be reading this a few years down the line, and the entertainment industry is blossoming beyond belief. I really hope that is the case. To everyone else out there, I hope that by the time this book makes its way to you we are leaps and bounds out of lockdown, and every person, household and business is thriving. If not, then keep looking for that light at the end of the tunnel.